Rejoicing In Life's "Melissa Moments"

The Joys Of Faith
And
The Challenges Of Life

Kenneth Cauthen

CSS Publishing Company, Inc., Lima, Ohio

REJOICING IN LIFE'S "MELISSA MOMENTS"

Copyright © 2002 by
CSS Publishing Company, Inc.
Lima, Ohio

All rights reserved. No part of this publication may be reproduced in any manner whatsoever without the prior permission of the publisher, except in the case of brief quotations embodied in critical articles and reviews. Inquiries should be addressed to: Permissions, CSS Publishing Company, Inc., P.O. Box 4503, Lima, Ohio 45802-4503.

Scripture quotations are from the *Revised Standard Version of the Bible*, copyrighted 1946, 1952, 1971, 1973, by the Division of Christian Education of the National Council of the Churches of Christ in the USA. Used by permission.

Library of Congress Cataloging-in-Publication Data

Cauthen, Kenneth, 1930-
 Rejoicing in life's "Melissa moments" : the joys of faith and the challenges of life / Kenneth Cauthen.
   p. cm.
 ISBN 0-7880-1944-9 (pbk. : alk. paper)
 1. Sermons, American. I. Title
 BV4253 .C38 2003
 252—dc21

2002013735

For more information about CSS Publishing Company resources, visit our website at www.csspub.com or e-mail us at custserv@csspub.com or call (800) 241-4056.

ISBN 0-7880-1944-9   PRINTED IN U.S.A.

To my grandson
Evan Freeman Cauthen-Brown
Born May 16, 2001

He will grow old
along with the century.

I wish them both well.

Table Of Contents

Preface   7

The Joys Of Faith
Rejoicing In Life's "Melissa Moments"   13
Lightning Bugs Over The Mudhole   21
The Gospel In Six Words   29
The Day God Cried   35
The Multiple Uses Of Grace   43

The Consolations Of Faith
Why Do We Suffer?   53
Consolation In Suffering   61
A Sermon For Saturday   69
The Cross-Shaped Scar In The Heart Of God   75

Living In A Complicated World
Is It Any Fun Being Good?   85
Living With The Weeds In The Wheat   93
The Reign Of Christ In A Complicated World   101
One Of These Days   109
Why Roman Soldiers Love The Sermon On The Mount   117

Peacemakers As Troublemakers
Jesus — That Troublemaker!   127
Two Ways To Get Crucified   135

Famous Unknowns I Have Known
Famous Unknowns	145
The Good Iranian	151
The Amazing Dr. Hobbs —	
And The Other Side Of The Story	159
The Deacons And The Demons	165

Communion
Risking Spirit	175
Memories, Memories, Memories	179

Authority And Freedom
On Using The Bible With Integrity	187
Holding On And Pressing On	195

Preface

These sermons are filled with stories from my own experience and from current events. Karl Barth once said that the preacher should go into the world with the Bible in one hand and a newspaper in the other hand. I have tried to follow that advice. The best preaching has always involved a lot of storytelling. Jesus set the example.

I have sought language that is simple, warm, and filled with feeling. I use the words of conversational speech as much as possible. The sermons included here are intended to speak to problems we confront in ordinary life. At the same time by training and profession I am a systematic theologian. I have taught for more than forty years in a theological seminary. I cannot and do not want to forget that when I write sermons. I have tried to make use of my specialized knowledge in interpreting the meaning of Scripture for today. For example, in the sermon "Why Roman Soldiers Love The Sermon On The Mount," I make reference to various ways the "hard sayings" of Matthew 5:38-43 have been interpreted in Christian history. Then I offer my own interpretation, which so far as I know is original with me. However, it would boost my own confidence to learn that others have found the distinction between the ethical and the ecstatic dimensions of love useful for dealing with this difficult passage.

I do not believe that profundity and obscurity require each other. Some deep ideas can be stated simply. At least, that is my goal. The compliment I like best is the one I have heard numerous times from laypeople: "Preacher, you really made us think today." In this way, I have tried to combine heart and head. But my students would tell you that I know the difference between the pulpit and the classroom. Increasingly, even as a professional theologian, I have attempted to discover the experiential meaning of the most theoretical of concepts. As a philosopher, I am a pragmatist. With William James I believe that the meaning of concepts is best understood when we can relate them to our life experiences.

A good deal of my professional life and writings has dealt with the problem of suffering in the light of faith. Many of these sermons reflect that interest. I have long been impressed with the fact that many of the issues we face in personal and social life are complex, yielding no simple answer. The solutions we offer are ambiguous, mixing good and evil, compelling us to live with many a trade-off. Many values are in tension with other values. To get something of what we want, we have to accept a lot we don't want. Several sermons reflect that awareness. Those who think there is a simple answer to every problem, and that we can make absolute distinctions between right and wrong in every instance, will not be happy with what they find in these pages.

As to method, it is fairly simple. I typically begin with a story out of everyday life. Then I go to the Bible and seek to find illumination of the meaning of these experiences. I use my theological training to mediate between the Bible and the newspaper. Two of my inspirations are pulpit masters from an earlier generation. Both taught me the same lesson. Halford Luccock, my homiletics professor at Yale, used to ask us this question: "What do you do when you get a group picture?" Answer: We all look at the picture to find ourselves in it. His point was that when people listen to sermons, their first concern is to see if they are in the picture. If they cannot find themselves, the preacher's cause is lost. Harry Emerson Fosdick once wrote that people do not come to church to find out what happened to the Jebusites. They come to see if there is a Word from the Lord mediated through the preacher that applies to them. That is why I begin nearly every sermon with a story from everyday life that concerns us all. I want to get the hearer and the reader in the picture from the start. It is not my purpose to do the theological equivalent of telling what happened to the Jebusites.

I have always been a "both and" rather than an "either or" thinker. These sermons seek to unite and include rather than separate and exclude aspects of life and experience. I attempt to combine humor and seriousness, joy and sadness, the tragic and the triumphant, realism and idealism, the cool head and the warm heart, analytical thought and deep feeling, simplicity and depth, religion and ethics, faith and reason, personal meaning and interpersonal morality, critical analysis and joyous proclamation, and so on. Above all, I have striven for complete integrity in dealing with the Scripture, Christian tradition, and the complexities of actual life in the streets, the home, the marketplace, and the political arena. It is my aim never to suppress any fact or dimension of life to protect churches, Christians, preachers, the Bible, or myself in the interests of sweetness and light when all is not sweetness and light. In one of my books I quote an author who says that no theological statement ought ever be made that cannot be made in the presence of burning children. I shudder to think about that, but I agree that the Christian community needs to make its affirmations about faith, hope, love, and the goodness of God while looking life right in the face with all its anxieties, terrors, and threats.

These sermons have been tested in churches and in the seminary chapel of Colgate-Rochester Divinity School. I have included here a collection of those my hearers have told me represent my best efforts. If these are my best, we need not go into the subject of what the others are like! They are offered to a wider audience for whatever value they may have for pastors and laypeople who may be interested to see how one preacher-theologian relates the Bible to the newspaper to get us all in the picture. How successful I have been, I will leave to others to judge.

Kenneth Cauthen
Rochester, NY
March 27, 2001

The Joys Of Faith

Rejoicing In Life's "Melissa Moments"

Matthew 17:1-8

What do you do with your mind when you are engaged in some routine task? How do you occupy yourself when washing dishes, mowing the lawn, or vacuuming the rug? I think about things — big things, little things, worrisome things, funny things, intellectual puzzles, practical problems. I reflect on whatever happens to pop into my head at the time. Of course, there may be a price to pay for this. Concentration on the task at hand may be diminished. Inadvertently you may not do the job as well as you might were you focused intently on what you are supposed to be doing. I myself have heard such remarks from my spouse as, "You didn't get this glass clean; orange pulp is clinging to the sides." My typical response is, "How can you be concerned about such trivial things? I almost resolved the ontological argument for the existence of God while I was almost washing that glass." There may be a cost for trying to think on the job. Yet the pleasure of getting some mental benefit out of what is merely routine is worth it — in most cases anyway.

Some years ago I was practicing the art of thinking-while-doing when I experienced a "Melissa moment." I was standing at the kitchen sink looking out the back window while washing the dishes. On this particular occasion I was engaged in some ruminations about a matter that often concerns me. Why, I asked myself, do I always seem to have mixed feelings about everything? Why am I always on the fence, leaning first this way and then the other? I seem to be of at least two minds about most things. I know so many difficulties with every possible solution to problems that I cannot get excited about any of them. I believe in a lot of things a little bit. I find it hard to believe in anything wholeheartedly. It worries me that I seem always to be overwhelmed by ambivalence, ambiguity, and complexity. It must be granted that being able to take into account all sides of issues is useful for some purposes. It is helpful in thinking about things. Whitehead was on the right track when he said, "All truths are half-truths." But going back and forth, seeing a little good everywhere, makes decision-making difficult. Finally, you have to do this or that. Thinking can make fine distinctions and assign proportionate validity to propositions. Helping students see that a theory accounts for some but not all the evidence can be useful in the classroom. I am good at that. But action is specific and definite. Will you vote for capital punishment or not? Is abortion to be a matter of freedom of conscience or a matter of legislation? Do you go for it when it is fourth down and inches to go, or do you kick the ball away? Do you get married or stay single? At vacation time do you go to the mountains or to the beach or to the big city? I was in the midst of some such cogitations at the time. I was feeling pretty depressed about my sense of always being on the boundary, betwixt and between, for and against every position, seeing a bit of truth in everything but finding the whole truth nowhere.

At that moment the front door burst open and in rushed a bundle of energy that moved quickly through the room and up the stairs. From the flurry of activity came a familiar voice. I heard these cheerful words, "Hi, Dad!" It was my daughter Melissa. As she bounded up the stairs to her room, I burst into tears with a great sense of relief. "Thank God, at least there are some things I don't have mixed feelings about." For if I know the deep interior of my heart, I feel for Melissa nothing but pure unbounded love, unqualified affection, and total joy. When I look back on that event, I call it "a Melissa moment." It was this same daughter who called me years later from Athens, Georgia. She began her conversation like this, "Hi, Dad, this is your daughter Melissa. Have you been hearing about the Freedom March today in Forsyth County? Well, I was there. I was too young during the '60s, so I wanted to be a part of this."

What is a "Melissa moment"? I mean those experiences now and then that bring clarity and conviction and assurance in the midst of situations otherwise riddled by ambiguity, ambivalence, confusion, and uncertainty. I mean those bright and shining moments which bring illumination and order into the midst of darkness and chaos. They are those times when we come to know who we are, what we believe, what we trust, and to what we are committed. They are those occasions on which we are unexpectedly surprised by joy with a simple reminder of what is unambiguously good and marvelous. A "Melissa moment" is any reordering of life that restores equilibrium and perspective, that refreshes and renews, that gets us back on track. Such experiences are precious. They are both revelatory and redemptive. They renew our motivation to get back into the thick of things to wrestle with stubborn facts that don't always fit into a neat pattern. They give us the courage to make choices and to do something that may make things a little better, although nothing we can do will make them perfect.

I need those moments. I struggle with faith and doubt. I live with ambiguity, ambivalence, and the necessity of compromise all the time. I read with envy the story of Sherwood Eddy. He was a wealthy philanthropist of a generation ago who supported many good causes that we would applaud. He was involved in getting Reinhold Niebuhr to Union Theological Seminary. He says that at one time he went through a period of great conflict, doubt, and despair. Then he had a great moment of transformation. He reports that he never had a moment's doubt about God since that time. I know there are people who have a once and for all sense of conviction about life and destiny. I am not among them. I feel more at home with those who live perpetually with a divided mind. I resonate with the sentiments conveyed by the father who brought his son to Jesus for healing. When told that faith would save his child, he cried out, "Lord, I believe; help my unbelief!" (Mark 9:24).

Moreover, it is not only in matters of faith that I struggle with mixed opinions. When it comes to ethics also, I find myself much less sure than many of my friends about the right course of action. Some people are just sure that nuclear power plants are nothing but pure evil, trouble in the making. Yet I sat in Boston at the World

Council of Churches Conference on Faith and the Future and heard two distinguished physicists debate the issue. They took opposing sides. One argued that given all the alternatives, the careful and cautious use of nuclear power is a reasonable choice. The other was convinced it was the path to sure ruin. If scientists from MIT can't agree, how can I choose intelligently? Did not the accident at Chernobyl settle all that? Maybe, but when the *Titanic* sank on its maiden voyage, should we have stopped building big ships? And the next time 50,000 people are killed on highways in one year, should we outlaw automobiles? Some of those who are so sure that nuclear power is of the devil seem to forget that thousands and thousands have died in coal mines during the last century. Many more will die if we continue to burn coal.

Moreover, I heard another scientist at MIT scare the daylights out of everybody talking about the dangers to health and safety involved in burning large amounts of coal. And we all know about the possible long-term dangers from using fossil fuels that might alter the climate with catastrophic consequences. If coal or nuclear energy pose such hazards, what are the alternatives? What should we be doing now? Who knows what is best? The situation seems awfully complex to me.

Some people are quite sure that abortion is murder pure and simple. Others are equally insistent that a woman's right to full control over her reproductive processes takes precedence over any rights the fetus might conceivably possess. Meanwhile, I agonize over the fact that both positions claim too much. I conclude that no resolution of this issue is available that does not seem to be about as much wrong as it is right. Either way suffering will result.

Some people seem to know that preferential policies to benefit groups previously excluded from jobs and other opportunities have all the right on their side. Others contend with equal vehemence for race- and sex-neutral policies that consider individuals as individuals. Am I wrong in thinking that most people take the position that is in their self-interest? Are the moral arguments and the ethical principles themselves decisive? I have a son and two daughters. All three will now and then be in the job market. As a parent, I hope that when Paul applies for a position, he will be considered on his own individual merits and not be treated as a member of a group. When my daughters are up for consideration, I hope they will be given preference because they are women. As a *parent* I hope for whatever benefits my children. As a *moral philosopher* trying to think clearly about the matter based on principles of justice, I find the situation to be fraught with all sorts of complexities and ambiguities. Neither policy is without negative features that border on injustice. Either policy hurts somebody. Both rest on sound ethical principles.

President Harry Truman wished that just once he could find a "one-handed" economist. Every time he called in the experts for advice, all he heard was that, *on the one hand*, option A would have thus and so benefits but would also have a number of unwanted consequences. *On the other hand*, option B would have a different set of good and bad outcomes. Reducing the capital gains tax might increase investment, but it is a gift to the rich. Raising the minimum wage benefits some but may cause others to lose their jobs. Measures to reduce inflation may increase unemployment. He got tired of all this "on the one hand" and "on the other hand" business. "Please give me a 'one-handed' economist," he pleaded.

We all wish for some "one-handed" moral advice on a lot of issues that baffle us. Unfortunately, life is complicated. Justice is not always totally and wholly on one side and injustice completely on the other side. Good and evil grow together like the wheat and the tares. If we are tossed about by many winds of doctrine, it may be because there is a little bit of truth in a lot of positions but not the whole truth in any. Our mixed feelings may simply represent the world as it is in all its stubborn and irreducible complexity.

So we need those "Melissa moments." In the midst of ambiguity it helps to be suddenly and unexpectedly surprised by something in which we can simply rejoice and celebrate with thanksgiving and praise to God. We need those times when complexity can be put aside so that we can wholeheartedly embrace the simple things that make us happy. We need those occasions when we can let go in an ecstatic and playful abandonment to something that makes our hearts sing. We need those hallelujah times now and then that lift our spirits to the heights. We need those periods of refreshing in which wrestling in grim solemnity with the moral perplexities of life gives way to moments of merriment and sheer enjoyment.

It helps if along the way we can have some "Melissa moments" that surprise us in the midst of our burdened seriousness with a revelation of what the heart really believes without reservation. Just when we think that there is nothing in life but uncertainty and weary striving, we are suddenly projected into those luminous moments in which we experience pure joy in something we knew all along but had forgotten in the midst of struggle and strife. In such times we can laugh at taking ourselves too seriously. We can see the comic elements where we had seen only tragedy. We can find peace and contentment even though the world is still full of suffering and absurdity.

Jesus said there is joy in heaven when even one sinner repents. Perhaps the angels rejoice also when some poor soul who frets too much about life's vicissitudes has a few moments of fun. In any case life on earth is impoverished without "Melissa moments." They give us a little time off from reforming the world and let us do a little crazy dancing. Life is dreary without experiences of renewal in which we stop worrying that the world is going to hell if we don't prevent it. Sometimes heaven itself may enjoin us to relax and be happy with the goodness that is right before us. Sometimes all it takes to put a spark back into our smile is a cheery "Hi, Dad" from a bundle of energy named Melissa.

It had been six days since Peter made his confession that Jesus was the Christ. Jesus took Peter, James, and John up a high mountain and was transfigured before them. His face shone like the sun. His garments became like white light. Moses and Elijah appeared with him. Whatever the origin of this story, it seems to have served the purpose of confirming the witness of Peter that the one now transformed before them was indeed the expected Messiah. Jesus was the long-awaited Savior sent from God. A voice came from the cloud and said, "This is my beloved Son, listen to him." Maybe they were startled by all this and didn't know what to say. Perhaps they thought the New Age had arrived finally. In any case, Peter spoke for them and said in effect, "Lord, if you want, we can make three booths and all stay here." This was not the right move. This experience of illumination and confirmation for the disciples could not be captured and held on to permanently. They had to get back to their preaching and healing.

So it is with the "Melissa moments" in our own lives. These transforming times on the mountain top are precious and wonderful beyond measure. They serve their purpose by preparing us for the journey back down the mountain into the world of stubborn facts, ambiguous moral choices, and the continuing struggle with suffering and injustice. These occasions when ordinary experience is transfigured provide the renewing and energizing grace that enables us to do the routine tasks of our witness and calling. Let us rejoice in life's "Melissa moments." They sustain us in the ordinariness of daily life when somebody has to wash the dishes.

Lightning Bugs Over The Mudhole

Psalm 103

The usual way is to speak of the problem of evil. How can there be so much misery and suffering in the world if God is both all-powerful and supremely good? It would appear either that God cannot or will not prevent or overcome suffering. If we say that God cannot, we question divine omnipotence. If we say God will not, we impugn God's love. Certainly the reality of evil is a fundamental problem for believers. It erodes the faith of many. Paul Tillich was a chaplain in World War I. He reported that the atheism he found among soldiers was most often rooted in their experience of massive suffering they experienced in the mud and blood of the trenches. You may have heard that there are no atheists in foxholes. Well, there are, and some of them become atheists by living in those very foxholes in the hell that war is.

The problem of evil is as real and threatening today. Misery, pain, and injustice are all around us. They are an ever present part of our consciousness. We remember Hitler and the slaughter of millions of Jews and other people. The very mention of Dresden, Pearl Harbor, and Hiroshima brings to mind the horror of modern war. We read about hunger and poverty on a global scale. Our television sets keep vividly before us the images of starving children. They are no more than skin and bones. Flies walk across dirty faces that display their inner agony. We can give specifics about the deep hatreds fermenting for centuries in the Middle East. Young Israeli soldiers shoot teenage Palestinians. Both groups are caught up in a demonic destructiveness they neither created nor can control. We are well acquainted with the threat of global extinction associated with nuclear war and ecological catastrophe. Newspapers tell us about earthquakes and hurricanes, cancer and babies with AIDS. We are not ignorant of hopelessness, murder, rape, child abuse, and the drug problem. We have read Camus, Kafka, and Beckett. Evil in all its forms continues to be a threat to our lives and to our faith.

It is hard to understand the giant agonies of the world if we believe in an Almighty Love. Nevertheless, it may be even more difficult to comprehend the goodness on earth if God is indifferent or impotent. Perhaps the greatest mystery of all is not that bad things happen to good and bad people alike. *Maybe the biggest puzzle is the surprising, unexpected, unexplainable, gratuitous fact of life itself and its potential for enjoyment.* What needs to be accounted for is the reality of pleasure, delight, and joy in the world. The problem of evil is urgent and inescapable. However, I want to turn the question around and deal instead with the problem of the good.

A friend of mine sent me an article he had written. The theme for the day is indicated by the title: "Fireflies in the Quagmire." Translated into a vocabulary reflecting my rural Georgia background, I ask, "Why are there lightning bugs flying over the mudhole?" Granted that the world is full of evil, nevertheless, how do we account for the good we experience in this life?

Take, first of all, the fact of existence itself. The most amazing, stupendous, inexplicable thing I know of is that I am, that I exist. A bedroom in the home of my parents in Georgia has a dresser in it that has been in the family as long as I can remember. It has a large central mirror with two smaller mirrors that fold in toward the middle. When I was a child, I used to amuse myself by standing in front of this dresser. I would pull the side mirrors against the back of my head and look at the endless reflections of reflections of myself that bounced off the three mirrors. After a while I would tire of that and look directly at myself eyeball to eyeball. Staring at myself at close range soon took on a kind of strangeness as all disappeared from my mind except the awareness of my awareness. I was conscious of nothing but being conscious. The mystery of this intrigued me. "Well, here I am, and I am really here. Why am

I here? Why does anything exist? Why is there something rather than nothing?" I did not know it at the time, but later I learned that I was exploring in my childlike way some of the fundamental questions of philosophy. At the moment I knew only the weirdness of it all. I felt the bare, stubborn fact of being there, of being alive, of being real. I experienced that fact in the odd feeling of being conscious of nothing but my own consciousness. So I put it before you that the starting point of all reflection about life is the sheer, factual givenness of our own existence.

The second fact is, if anything, even more mysterious. I am, and it is good to be. I do not mean that nothing evil ever happens. Of course, life can sometimes be utterly miserable. All I mean is that the promise of life is good. As the philosopher in me would put it, life is potentially and essentially good when seen as a whole and its fullest dimensions.

Saint Augustine wrote a great deal that I find abhorrent, simply awful. On one point I find him the most excellent and eloquent witness I know. No one exceeded him in extolling the goodness of creation. In a magnificent passage he exclaims that there is something so infinitely sweet about the sheer fact of existing that even those who are miserable wish not to perish but to know relief from their suffering. Does not every animal, from the largest dragon down to the smallest worm, show by every movement and action possible that it wishes to stay alive? And do not even the plants send their roots deep into the earth and their leaves outward to the sun so that they may live and grow?

That insight of Saint Augustine is affirmed in our own experience. We feel it in our own awareness that life holds the promise of pleasure, joy, and moments of ecstasy. I remember an occasion more than three decades ago when the goodness of life broke into my own awareness with particular vividness. It was for me a rare moment of mystical ecstasy. I was walking from a classroom at Emory University to my apartment. It was one of those crisp days in March when the cloudless sky was totally blue. The sun was shining in all its Georgia brightness. The mixture of warmth and coolness told all that spring was already awakening the dormant earth. I walked through a grove of pine trees and heard the wind softly breathing through the thick branches. All of a sudden and unexpectedly, I felt a surge of good feeling. It can only be described as an acute, deep awareness of the pure joy of being alive. It was as if the pine trees and all of nature shared the experience. All around me was the busy world of living and dying. Not far away was a little shopping center where people bought food, clothes, and medicine. About a block in the distance was Emory Hospital where people of all ages and of all races and of all stations in life were suffering and dying. The world in all of its beauty and pain was still there. Nevertheless, in my little cathedral in the pines I knew for a brief few moments what it meant for Genesis to proclaim that God looked at the world still fresh and pure and saw that it was good, very good.

What I felt is confirmed in those simple joys of everyday life. Think about the experience of loving and of being loved, the sound of a good ragtime band playing the music of Scott Joplin, the thrill of achievement and success, the taste of honey, and the refreshing touch of a cool breeze on a hot day. A thousand other simple pleasures testify to the goodness of life. I see a similar witness in the play of puppies, in the luxurious stretch of a cat fresh from a nap, in the persistent effort of sprouting seeds to find their way around every obstacle on their journey toward the sun, in the curiosity of babies that leads them to explore the world they have so recently entered, and in the first smiles they offer to loving parents. These and countless other down-to-earth spontaneous reactions of animals and people tell us that the best things in life are free.

Let us grant that when things go wrong, life can be agony. Existence can be miserable. Living can be hell on earth that at its worst becomes despair itself. But when all goes right, the promise of life can be realized in a sweet taste of exquisite enjoyment. When life is lived in a healthy body in a just society in loving communion with others, life can be splendid indeed. Living is intrinsically good. Existing is worthwhile beyond the power of words to express. My favorite philosopher — Alfred North Whitehead — says that all life is driven by a three-fold urge "to live, to live well, and to live better." Life in all its forms instinctively affirms its inherent goodness by its tenacious efforts to stay alive and to improve the quality of existence.

Why should life be good? Why should existence even offer the promise of enjoyment? That is the mystery. How amazing that there should be fireflies in the quagmire! How stupendous that lightning bugs fly over the mudhole!

A third surprising fact of life gives rise to wonder. It is a little more difficult to describe. Yet it takes us close to the heart of Christian faith. I speak now of the experience of grace. I refer to that overplus of life-renewing mercy, joy, and strength that appears in the darkness to enable us to rise up from defeat and despair and to go on at the rising of the sun. Grace means unmerited favor. It means the gift that overcomes the power of evil and makes possible the triumph of the good. I speak here of the resurrection that follows crucifixion, of forgiveness that overcomes enmity and betrayal. I point to the reversal of reversal, the defeat of defeat, of the dawn that comes unexpectedly when it had seemed like the night would go on forever. In a word, I speak of the Easter experience. Jesus was dead and buried, but on the third day, he rose again. Israel was in Egypt, slaves in bondage, but God sent Moses to deliver them. The younger son came home in poverty and disgrace, but his father embraced him in loving forgiveness and said, "This my son was dead, but now is alive again; let us rejoice and be merry." A woman was taken in adultery, and some wanted to stone her. But Jesus said, "I do not condemn you; go and sin no more." Rosa Parks refused to go to the back of the bus. God sent Martin Luther King, Jr., to lead a movement for justice so that the Rosa Parks of the world would never have to go to the back of the bus ever again.

I could tell you of dark moments in my own life when I was not sure life had meaning anymore. Hope appeared to be dead forever. Finally, relief came. Joy returned as a surprise from heaven that I cannot explain but can only confess in gratitude. Now I invite you to add your own experiences of grace. Can you remember some moment in life when all seemed lost? Can you recall the victory that was given from beyond? Didn't it feel like a gift that comes as a surprise?

We are coming close to the heart of the gospel. The New Testament is all about grace, justification, liberation by a power from beyond, the triumph of suffering love, forgiveness for the sinner, reconciliation for the estranged, new hope for the despairing, new life for those trapped in despair. How uncalled for! Amazing grace! Amazing, wondrous grace! How did these fireflies get in the quagmire?

What are we to make of all this? How are we to account for the startling fact that we are at all? How can we explain the astounding awareness that the promise of life is good? How can we make sense of the experience of grace that brings light when darkness might have been expected to grow deeper? Let me suggest to you that in the Christian tradition, coming to terms with these deep mysteries of life is what God-talk is all about. The Christian who speaks of God is pointing to the Creator and the Redeemer, the giver of life and the savior of life. To believe in God is to have confidence in our hearts that we exist by the operation of some power beyond us. It is acknowledgment that we have the capacity for enjoyment as a gift of a goodness that we neither created nor can control. It is the affirmation that we are renewed by grace that freely breaks into life to surprise us with joy. To talk about God is to witness to the unfathomable mystery at the depth of things, the power that creates us, the justice that judges us, and the love that redeems us. To know God is to encounter the creativity that, without our knowledge or consent, bestows the gift of life and renews its possibilities with fresh energies and graces that keep us going.

I would not claim that the author of Psalm 103 was reflecting on exactly the same sorts of experiences that I have been enumerating. Rather I dare to think that I have been continuing the meditation on existence that the Psalmist was engaging in. This poetic soul looked at life and concluded that at the heart of all things is a Loving Kindness who created the world and all that is in it, who redeems life when it hits bottom. The ultimate fact is a Gracious Presence who forgives iniquity, who heals diseases, who crowns our heads with steadfast love and mercy. We are frail, weak, foolish, sinful, and mortal, but our Creator pities us as good parents have compassion for their children. Human existence is like grass that flourishes for a moment and then perishes; human flesh is like dust that the wind will soon carry away. Underneath and all around are the Everlasting Arms. Confronting the mystery of life before its Creator, the Psalmist was led to cry out with joy, "Bless the Lord, O my soul; and all that is within me, bless his holy name!" (Psalm 103:1). When we see the lightning bugs over the mudhole, what else can we say but, "Bless the Lord, O my soul"?

How does it happen that we are? Why is it good to be? Where does saving grace come from? To deal with these mysteries in the church is to talk about, to believe in, and to worship the God of Abraham and Sarah, of Rebekah and Isaac, and of Jacob and Rachel. To reflect upon the coming to be and passing away of the flesh that is like grass is to acknowledge the God of Psalm 103. To have faith in this Creator-Redeemer is to trust in the One in whom Jesus trusted. How did the fireflies get in the quagmire? There can be only one answer: "Bless the Lord, O my soul; and all that is within me, bless his holy name!" (Psalm 103:1).

The Gospel In Six Words[1]

Romans 5:6-11; 1 Corinthians 1:18-31

Bradley wanted to be good for nothing. His mother was. That was sufficient for him. This is how it came about. Bradley was a little boy. One morning he came to breakfast and laid a note on his mother's plate. The note said: "Mother owes Bradley, for running errands, $.25; for being good, $.10; for taking music lessons, $.15; extras, $.05; total, $.55." At lunch time Bradley found some change on his plate that totaled $.55. He was excited and pleased that his initiative had worked so well. There was also a note with the money, which he picked up and read. The note said: "Bradley owes Mother, for being good, $.00; for nursing him through his long illness with scarlet fever, $.00; for all his meals and a beautiful room, $.00." Bradley's little eyes filled with tears. He gave the money back. He reached out to hold his mother in a tight embrace. Finally, he said to her, "Take all the money back, Mama, and let me love you and do things for nothing."[2]

Christians are good for nothing. Yes, but we must understand what is meant. We do not suggest that they serve no useful purpose in the world. Perhaps some don't, but the real ones are good for a lot of things. At their best, Christians are the salt of the earth, the light of the world, the yeast in the dough. They introduce into life more of the love the world needs now. Christians are good for nothing in the sense that they don't have to be paid to love each other and to do good things for those in need. They love because they have first been loved. Their love to God and for each other springs out of gratitude for the gift of love they have known in their own lives. In summary, that is what the gospel is all about.

Some of us remember those old radio contests in which we tried to win a prize by describing something "in 25 words or less." We still use the phrase to demand of each other a brief answer to a question. We preachers talk about the gospel. What is the gospel in 25 words or less? It would be foolish for anyone to think it possible to reduce the richness of the good news to a few propositions. Yet I suggest that we need only six words to get at the heart of it. *God loves you. Love one another.* What this means is that Christianity is all about love, divine love and human love and all about the connections divine and human love have with each other. To put the same thing in different terms, the gospel proclaims a gift — the gift of divine love. The gospel announces a demand — the demand that we love each other with the same quality of love with which God has first loved us. The gospel revolves around and around this double center: God loves you. Love one another.

Much could be said in spelling all this out. To do so with the depth and eloquence the subject deserves requires greater gifts than I possess. I want to make one main point. *Until we have experienced the gift of love, we cannot meet the demand of love.* When we have been assured deep in our hearts that we are loved, loving another becomes possible. Love will flow out from us as a spontaneous expression of the joy and gratitude that fills our being.

Whenever I see people who are bitter and full of hate, I conclude that at some significant point in their lives they were never loved. Or they were not convinced that they were loved by those who counted most. Time and again when some gunman goes berserk and kills a lot of people, it turns out the murderer has lived through some terrible times as a child. Many such tragic souls were beaten, abandoned, or mistreated in some way. Either their parents gave them very mixed signals about whether they loved them, or they had been shifted from one foster home to another, or something of the sort. Again and again people who have these outbursts of hatred and go wild with violence look back to periods when they desperately needed to be loved and remained unloved.

A young man in Montreal killed fourteen women and then turned the gun on himself. The report said he was abandoned at age seven by his father when his parents separated. He suffered in other ways as well. He was turned down for the military. He had known a lot of failure and rejection. It happens again and again that people who are unloved or unwanted or cruelly treated as children grow up to be violent adults. Anyone not assured of being loved is a lost person. He or she may be dangerous and vicious with little or no provocation. The only way you can save someone like this is to convince him or her somehow that somebody who matters cares, that somebody loves them despite everything.

Next time a schoolboy or an adult takes a gun and kills family members, business associates, or murders randomly, look for the follow-up stories. Again and again, we learn of a childhood marked by parental divorce, abuse, neglect, abandonment, or other features of a life without sufficient love from those who count most. Or you will learn of a threat of the loss of love from a spouse seeking a divorce or some other frustration that makes that person desperate from lack of the comforts of sufficient supporting love where it matters most.

This brings us to one of the most fundamental facts about human life. It leads us directly into the meaning of the cross of Jesus of Nazareth. *We need to be loved most when we deserve it least.* We need to be loved most at the very time that others find it difficult to love us. Unless there is some way to set in motion a redemptive flow of love to someone who needs it but does not deserve it, there is no salvation from the destructive chain of reverberating hate. This is precisely the point at which the Christian proclamation becomes gospel, becomes good news.

Paul writes in his letter to the Romans that God shows love for us in that while we were sinners, Christ died for us. Grace — that is the good news. The gift of love goes forth to those who need it desperately but don't deserve it. The person who has received the gift of love can begin to meet the demand of love. What is true about the relationship between God and humanity holds equally true for our human relationships.

How can we break the vicious cycle by which evil reproduces itself in a never-ending chain of cause and effect? The only way is for some person or some group to find the spiritual resources to return love for hate, tenderness for cruelty, to forgive instead of retaliating, to bless those who curse, to repay good for evil. Somebody somewhere has got to love somebody else when he or she doesn't deserve to be loved. This means there is redemptive power in suffering love. This is what the Christian witness to the cross of Jesus is all about. God exercises saving power only by becoming powerless on the cross. This is the foolishness of the cross about which Paul speaks. God's love is suffering love. The foolishness is the claim that only powerless love has power to save, that suffering love can end suffering. Consider Jesus of Nazareth hanging helpless on a cross praying, "Father, forgive them, for they know not what they do." Observe Martin Luther King, Jr., watching a state trooper kick at one of his children in Mississippi, saying, "Don't do that, Mister. It will only cause trouble." The tough cynic is bound to say, "If that is all there is to count on in this world, then God sure is in a bad way."

Harry Emerson Fosdick, the great preacher of a generation ago, tells of someone speaking to a group of derelicts at a Rescue Mission in New York City. He was talking about the prodigal son who squandered his inheritance. When he returned home in shame, he was met by his father with outstretched hands. The preacher went on to relate how the son was forgiven. He told how he was received back into the household. He noted that a party was planned to celebrate the occasion. When he got to the part about the singing and dancing, one of the weather-beaten old men in the audience said, "So he put it over on the Old Man again, did he?" That is the way the gospel of forgiveness sounds to a hard-bitten, cynical world.

When Martin Luther King, Jr., was killed, militants in the black community wasted no time in pointing to his dead body as more evidence of the futility of non-violent suffering love. The only alternative, they said, is for black people to arm themselves and fight back.

Yet there is a deeper wisdom in the foolishness of suffering love that keeps on seeking our allegiance. People need to be loved most when they deserve it least. The further truth is that only as they find themselves being loved anyway, can they can begin to recover from the sickness of self-centeredness. Only one who has received the gift of love can love another. The Christian proclamation is that God loves us and that we ought to love one another. The heart of Christian preaching is this: Receive the gift, and you can begin to meet the demand. Those who feel deeply and unconditionally loved by God and by those who matter to them on earth will want in return to be good for nothing.

Dr. E. Stanley Jones tells the story of a government worker in India whose work often took him away from home. In his loneliness he became unfaithful to his wife. He was a morally sensitive man and could not endure this stain on his conscience. One day he summoned the courage to tell the whole story to his wife. When the meaning of his words began to dawn on her, she turned pale and stumbled against the wall. Relating this story, the man said, "In that moment I saw the meaning of the cross. I saw love crucified by sin." Because his wife loved him very deeply, she forgave him. They began a new life together.

Love crucified by sin — that often happens to love. Yet there is saving power in crucified love that can reach into the heart of a guilt-ridden, hate-filled soul and heal it in a way that nothing else can. The external constraints of the law, the enforcing power of the bayonet, and the prudent wisdom of enlightened self-interest can bring about a form of order and a kind of minimum justice in society. But the healing of the heart from inside is a miracle that can be wrought only by the transforming energy of crucified love. Do we have the wisdom to believe in this foolishness?

---

1. An earlier version of this sermon was published with the title "The Gift and Demand of Love" in *Pulpit Digest* (April 1969), pp. 21-24. Reprinted with permission from *Pulpit Digest*, copyright Logos Productions Inc. (800-328-0200).

2. Adapted from John A. Redhead, *Getting To Know God* (Nashville: Abingdon Press, 1954), p. 121.

The Day God Cried

Romans 1:18-32; 3:23-26; 5:6-11
1 Corinthians 1:18-25

She was only sixteen years old when the court sentenced her to death for her crime. She and two or three other teenage girls had attacked and killed an old woman. They broke into her house. They kicked, stabbed, and beat her viciously and without mercy until she died. As I listened to the story, I felt a growing rage within me. How could anyone be so cruel, so insensitive, so callous, and so mean? How could they listen to her pleas for mercy and not be touched? They set upon the old woman who had done nothing to them and assaulted her body until she fell to the floor. The poor soul died repeating the Lord's Prayer. The ring leader of the group was fifteen years old at the time. She was caught, tried, found guilty, and sentenced to die. As I heard the story — let me be candid — I was so angry with her despite her youth that I almost wanted to strangle her myself. The premeditated viciousness and cruelty were totally unprovoked and without cause. I felt all my convictions against the death penalty being tested. Are there not some crimes so monstrous that those who commit them forfeit their membership in the human community? I was outraged and wrathful that these heartless girls could continue to stab and beat an old woman who was pleading for mercy and praying to God.

A few minutes later I was watching this young woman being interviewed. First of all, it was the look on her face that got to me. It was an expression of such sadness and tragedy that, despite what she had done, I felt my heart softening a bit. She said she didn't want to die. She wanted to live out her normal span of years. She began to tell the story of her own life. She had been mistreated and abused in her own home. She spoke of how ashamed she was of her family situation. They seemed different somehow. Here was a vulnerable, sensitive child who needed love and security in her own tender years and had not received it. I sat there watching her and listening. The sorrow and pain on her face broke through my rage. A large tear formed in each eye and slowly ran down her cheek.

What inner pain and humiliation she must have known in her early years. It all came to the surface now and was plainly revealed in the expression on her face. She had done a vicious thing and had been sentenced to die for it. Her young life appeared to be headed for a tragic end. She had never known how good life can be when you are loved and cared for by those who matter most. I shall never forget the look on her face. A few minutes ago, I had been ready to strangle her. Now I was moved to tears of my own and wanted to reach out in compassion and let her know that somebody cares. There but for the grace of God and love of family and friends — especially in those early years — go we all.

It was a rather remarkable experience for me. I went from wrath and rage to mercy and compassion toward one human being. She was a cruel murderer. She was also a precious young life whose own spirit had been crushed by people and powers beyond her control when she needed to be loved and nourished.[1]

I came to a new appreciation of Paul's letter to the Romans that day. The apostle does not begin with any sentimentality about a liberal, warm-hearted deity who overlooks our wrongdoing as if it did not matter much. No namby-pamby, teddy bear, wimp of a God here. This is no tearful bleeding heart who is so concerned for the perpetrator of violence that the victim is forgotten. Instead, we are told in thundering terms that the Almighty is full of fierce anger at rebelliousness and unrighteousness. The wrathful deity of Romans 1 is the God the visiting evangelist would hold up before the fourth grade Sunday school class during the revival meeting. That would soften them up for the altar call later during the preaching service, as we sang the invitation hymn.

Just listen to Paul for a moment. The wrath of God is revealed from on high against all the ungodliness and wickedness of humanity ... Sinners are without excuse; they know better. And since they did not see fit to pay attention to God, God gave them up to a base mind and to improper conduct. They were filled with all manner of wickedness, evil, covetousness, malice, full of envy, murder, strife, deceit, malignity; they are gossips, slanderers, haters of God, insolent, haughty, boastful, inventors of evil, disobedient to parents, foolish, faithless, heartless, ruthless. Though they know God's decree that those who do such things deserve to die, they not only do them, but approve those who practice them (Romans 1:18-32).

One has the impression that Paul was writing rapidly at the end of this first chapter, putting down whatever came to mind. The point was not to make a complete list of the sins of the race but to illustrate the fact that humanity is in bad trouble with Almighty God. We have made a mess of the world. The divine law has been violated. God is full of wrath at what we have done. While thinking and writing about all this, one gets the feeling that Paul was getting all worked up and infuriated himself. He was getting madder and madder at wicked sinners.

Yet only a couple of pages later, we seem to be in a completely different world. Now we are told that despite the fact that we come short of the glory of God, we are justified by grace as a gift through the redemption that is in Jesus Christ. This gift is to be accepted in grateful love and simple trust. We are saved by grace through faith. The astounding good news is that God shows love for us in that while we were yet sinners, Christ died for us (Romans 3:23-36; 5:6-11). Amazing grace, how sweet the sound, that saves the wretches of the world who have turned earth into hell. What boundless love, what infinite mercy, what tender compassion this is. The good news is that wrath is not the last word; grace is. The final verdict is that love will not let us off, will not let us down, will not let us go.

Christian faith is born in a paradox. This does not imply that it is based on a logical contradiction. It means that Christian preaching witnesses to something contrary to what we would have expected. Wrath and hot anger are overcome by suffering love. Forgiveness is offered to us as a gift to those who do not deserve it.

I have raised a lot more questions with all this heavy theology and the tragic story with which I began than I will answer. There is, for example, the terribly difficult question of how free and responsible we are for our actions. Every fiber of my being wants to say that we are accountable for what we do, no matter what our childhood was like. But I am not sure that in every instance we have the power to choose otherwise than we do. Just as a bridge can hold up only so much weight, maybe our human frame can bear only so much and beyond that collapses into actions that are beyond our control. A few tragic souls may have become so broken down by their past that they have lost most of their capacity to decide between alternatives. They may be nearly enslaved to the demons that rage within. In any case, I am pretty sure that some people have a greater range of choice than others.

One thing has impressed me. Again and again when the newspapers report some horrible crime that is truly outrageous, the follow-up articles on the childhood backgrounds reveal a similar pattern. Time after time it turns out that these violent people have themselves been victims of violence. Parents who mistreat their children have often themselves been abused. Assassins and murderers have frequently known childhood experiences in which they were beaten or neglected or felt themselves deeply humiliated and unloved.

I state no universal laws. I excuse no person or group who commits acts of cruelty and terror. Certainly I make no declarations that all wrongdoing can be traced to particular causes. I do not assert that all who sin have been sinned against in equal or worse ways. I suspect that the truth is both more simple and more complicated than all the theories the theologians and psychologists have ever put forward.

Let us take another example. For a while back in 1985 we were all preoccupied with the hijacking of a TWA airplane in which passengers were held captive. One of the hostages later confessed that the experience had given him an education regarding the conflict between the Israelis and the Arabs. From the hijackers he had learned that the Arabs have legitimate points to make. All that struck a responsive chord in me because my education was advanced a bit also during this period. Those responsible for the hijacking were Shiites. In many Arab countries the Shiites have been a minority. They have often been oppressed, abused, shunned, and, in general, badly treated. Many of them are poor and desperate. It is out of this kind of background that some of them have turned to violence and terrorism.

A small group of people did some terrible things. They took innocent people on an airplane and held them hostage. One person was beaten and killed. At the same time, the perpetrators of violence themselves have a history of persecution, oppression, and bad treatment. I am not pretending to have instant expertise on these matters. The issues go back for centuries. They are complex, many-sided. All parties have legitimate complaints and valid claims. Probably no group has as much truth and justice in their camp as they maintain.

The question I want to press is this: What attitude should we take toward people who do awful things to others? How should we treat those who rape, murder, torture, and mistreat without mercy? What shall we do with adults who physically and sexually abuse children, punish them without mercy, starve them, and do all sorts of other vicious and heartless things? In particular, how should we deal with such people when we discover that they have themselves been the victim of violence? Does the letter to the Romans have anything to teach us? I think it may. In fact, we have in the paradoxical combination of wrath and love that overcomes wrath just the combination we need.

First of all, when horrible crimes of murder, rape, and violence are committed, it is appropriate to be wrathful. Those who do such things must be held accountable. A civilized and decent world cannot tolerate such lawlessness. There may be a place for retribution in some appropriate fashion at the level of an eye for an eye and a tooth for a tooth in the crazy, absurd world in which we live. Wrath is the side of love that comes into play when violence is done to the children of God.

Beyond wrath, however, is forgiving love. This is the hard part. Let no one tell you it is easy. When God forgives us, there is a cost to pay. There is suffering. Love suffers when it forgives. That is the meaning of the cross. That is what all that talk about being saved by the blood of Jesus is about, all that talk about expiation for sin, all that talk about Christ dying for us. When we forgive one another, we suffer. To forgive means to bear the hurt the other has caused and burn it out in cross-bearing love. We must accept the evil inflicted on us and suffer through it until wrath has been consumed by love. Only then are we able to set the perpetrator free.

And what about the terrorists? We hear a lot about punishing the perpetrators. If we are to follow the way of the cross, there is more to it than that. A first step is to ask whether violence is a desperate measure to call attention to injustice. Love will seek justice for all. The surprising thing is that treating everyone fairly may be the only way to end violence. Unless somebody, somewhere, somehow is able to love beyond wrath, the vicious cycle of terror will go on and on. In the long run love may be the only thing that works.

Walter Wangerin, Jr., tells of an episode in his family life. He caught his young son Matthew stealing comic books from the local library. He was appalled that his own offspring would do such a thing. Various things were tried to make him stop. Matthew got a stern lecture from the librarian, Mrs. Outlaw. But it kept happening. Finally, in desperation Walter felt he had to punish the boy. So he turned Matthew across his lap and paddled his little bottom and then rushed out into the hall in tears. He eventually composed himself and came back into the room and held his little boy, telling him how much he loved him and how much he hated to punish him.

Years later, Matthew and his mother were in the car returning from a shopping center. They talked about old times. The comic book incident came into the conversation. He asked his mother if she knew why he quit stealing the comic books. "Yes," she replied. "Your father punished you." "No," he protested. "That's not the reason. I quit because Daddy cried."[2] It was not the wrath of Matthew's father that was effective. It was the suffering love of old dad who could not stand to paddle his child, even though he was mad at the child for stealing. It was not punishment that brought about repentance and new life. It was Daddy's tears.

While the world goes about seeking revenge and prescribing force and retaliation, here are those silly Christians going all over the place pointing to a cross and preaching about the day God cried. God demonstrates love for us in that while we were still sinners, Christ died for us (Romans 5:8). This is the foolishness of the cross. Oh, it's true that wrath and law and punishment have a preliminary work to do. But the folly of the word we preach is that ultimate redeeming power is suffering love. The most powerful force for redemptive change in those who do wicked deeds is not fear of punishment but that they come to know in their hearts that despite everything they are deeply loved by those they have offended. God still cries for wayward children, and in that example is to be found the clue to how we must act toward those who act unjustly if we are to save them and us from perpetual conflict and strife.

---

1. The preceding paragraphs were originally published in *The Many Faces Of Evil*, CSS Publishing Co., Lima, Ohio, 1997, pp. 41-42. Used by permission.

2. Walter Wangerin, Jr., *The Manger Is Empty: Stories In Time* (San Francisco: Harper & Row, 1989), pp. 116-132.

The Multiple Uses Of Grace

Ephesians 2:1-10

You may have made use of a household oil having the brand name "3 in 1." It claims to clean, oil, and polish. When I was a teenager, I heard a preacher use this product as an analogy to the Trinity. He went on to indicate three ways God functions. I did not know it in those innocent days, but I later learned that this way of thinking about the Trinity is heretical. Nevertheless, the idea of something having multiple uses always arouses interest. Grace falls into this category.

We are most familiar with the idea that grace saves us from our sins. It is not by our good works but by the free gift of forgiveness that we become acceptable in God's sight. Salvation by grace through faith was a central theme of the Protestant Reformation. To be set free from the burden of having to measure up to the high demands of divine law by the unmerited favor of God's mercy is not only amazing but a source of "Blessed Assurance."

Oh, we have our problems in keeping faith itself from becoming a new work that substitutes for keeping the law. And we sometimes quantify it as if faith were something we must somehow summon up enough of to make it work. And, yes, we have difficulty accepting grace deep in our hearts as well as in our heads. As a result we go about still burdened with guilt and condemnation and feelings of worthlessness. Even those of us who have preached grace to others have sometimes been unable to believe that we really are set free by an unconditional love that we do not have to earn. We may sing, "Just as I am, without one plea," but we often act and feel as if we had to be perfect or be damned. Nevertheless, our confession is that we are saved by grace.

Grace also saves us from our uncertainty about ultimate truth and our doubts about ultimate goodness. A London taxi driver recognized that the person who was getting into his cab was none other than Bertrand Russell, the great philosopher. He told the following story about his encounter with his famous passenger. "I said to him, 'Sir Bertrand, what's it all about?' And, you know, he couldn't tell me." Well, Bertrand Russell is not the only one who suffers from this disability. None of us knows for sure "what it's all about." We cannot decipher the deepest mysteries of existence. The final facts about the origin and destiny of the universe are beyond our ken.

More serious is the difficulty of believing that the ultimate power that rules all is perfect goodness. Such confidence is not easy in a world so full of suffering and injustice. Can grace save us from the despair of finding no meaning as well as from the guilt of not doing the good? Maybe grace is even that amazing.

Living by grace is trusting that the great unknown will not be destructive of our worthy hopes. Grace lets us embrace the mystery in the confidence that in the final reckoning the absurdities and sufferings of this life will not annihilate our just aspirations. On our part the ability to believe in spite of everything to the contrary is assisted by the goodness we do experience. When we cast ourselves upon the sea of life in the trust that the final mysteries are merciful, we can be tranquil in the turbulence and somehow manage to cope with the glimmers of significance that are available to us.

Grace enables us to acknowledge the big mystery that is beyond us and to live with the small meanings that are available. Our ignorance about ultimates does not imply that our flickering insights and occasional intuitions are worthless. Seeing through a glass darkly only means we cannot see all things clearly. It does not mean that we see nothing at all.

Some other uses of grace may not be so familiar. Yet I want to suggest that grace not only saves us from our sin and from our doubt but also from our bafflement. One of the features of moral decision-making in our time is that it frequently involves a highly technical dimension to which only experts can speak. Even if we ask the experts, we don't get one clear answer from them. They are divided on many things. Someone said that if you laid all the economists in the world end to end, they would not add up to one sure conclusion. Another thing about experts is that they have political and moral commitments that may influence their advice. It is hard to know sometimes where their technical expertise ends and their personal value system begins.

Most politicians have moral beliefs, but they also ask which position will get them the most votes. That makes it difficult for us to trust them. Just look at their panic today when the political winds regarding abortion seem to blow strongest first one way and then another. Some Democrats who have been for campaign finance reform are having second thoughts now that they have been able to raise as many dollars as the Republicans from "soft money." Another complication is that where people are in the social hierarchy influences their outlook on things. Does anyone believe that the point of view someone holds about whether the capital gains tax should be reduced is a matter of pure economic theory and not also a matter of political preference and self-interest?

Nevertheless, even when we have deciphered the political inclinations of the experts and unmasked the political pressures of the politicians, many problems are still baffling. Some of them are just complex and admit no simple solution. What are we to do about the possibility that the continued burning of fossil fuels on a massive scale may alter the global climate with catastrophic results? Illegal drugs are on everybody's mind these days. Does anyone know a good way out of the impasse? Part of the predicament is that a lot of issues involve so many painful trade-offs. We are always in a quandary because we can gain some good only at the expense of bringing some evil along with it. Raising the minimum wage assists those who are on the low end of the wage scale, but it may increase unemployment. Some years ago the Supreme Court ruled that it was unconstitutional for the state of Oregon to ban the use of peyote in the religious services of the Native American

Church. That violates religious freedom. Yet the use of peyote is illegal for all citizens in that state.

We have good reason to be puzzled about the best thing to do. We should add that the moral enterprise is most bewildering of all for those who really seek justice for all instead of acting instinctively on the basis of some unquestioned doctrine or merely out of narrow self-interest.

Today many Christians are puzzled and almost dazed wanting to do what is right but not sure what that implies. What would it involve to be freed gracefully from bafflement? First of all, we would be freed from the necessity and burden of knowing the whole truth all the time. This would enable us to act positively on the best we can figure out for now without claiming that we are absolutely right or without conceding that we have no basis for an opinion at all.

Finally, grace may create a confidence to act decisively even when we are about as uncertain as we are certain. If one option seems to us relatively better, all things considered, we have to go with that. We have no choice but to act on the best that we know up to now. We can proceed even zealously in the awareness that others are acting on insights different or contrary to ours that will get into the picture what we either cannot see or even object to. Beyond that we live in hope that, out of the efforts of all, some providence working beyond our ken will weave some pattern of meaning and goodness that will increase harmony and happiness on this earth. Yes, grace may be so amazing that it can save us from our bafflement.

One final use of grace remains. Here the test is even more severe. Yet I dare propose that grace can save us even from our morality, from our convictions, from our certainty, from our good works. I do not have access to that Great Computer in the sky. If I did, I would submit as a proposition to be tested that a good portion of the misery in this world has been caused by people who were pretty sure they were doing God's will.

Martin Marty tells of a young priest who was reporting to the bishop an experience he had at an ecumenical wedding. The priest saw a group of non-Catholics coming toward him to receive communion. Should he serve them? So he asked himself, "What would Jesus do?" Immediately the bishop interrupted. "You didn't serve them, did you?" Marty reflects that we are usually pretty sure how we want those "What would Jesus do?" stories to turn out. Ah, it may be that right here grace falters. But unless grace can save us from our good works, from our moral certainty, from our righteousness, we may be lost after all. The sin of us preachers may be our certainty about what the gospel really is. The sin of us professors may be our confidence that we understand things divine. The sin of preachers, priests, bishops, archbishops, cardinals, popes, and church convention presidents may be the certitude that they instruct and administer on the basis of traditions divinely authorized. We speak now of the sin of the good, decent people who are sure they have marked out a path that God not only approves but has ordained.

Karl Barth was once accosted by a critic who asked why he must always be right. Barth is reported to have replied, "But I always am right." Fortunately, the great theologian believed more than most of us in the triumph of grace in human life. Maybe grace can even save him from statements like that, assuming that he meant to be taken seriously, which is not at all certain. Doubtless, surprises will abound on Judgment Day. I suspect that those who will be most surprised are those who think they know what the surprises are to be.

We could all make our lists, couldn't we? We all have our inventory of those who have done evil in the name of good. In our catalogues would be those theologians of the nineteenth century who proved by the Bible and quoted Aristotle to show that slavery was permissible. On our lists would be all those theologians and preachers from the New Testament era until now who have put women in a place inferior to men. Good Pope John Paul II would be there with his guarantee that unnatural birth control and women priests are contrary to divine intention. Oh, yes, we could all make our index of errors. I am sure you see already the trap into which we are about to fall. When I make my directory of those other people who do evil in the name of good, I am saying that while they thought they knew what Jesus would do, they were wrong. But I and all who agree with me know what Jesus really would do. Perhaps the deepest difficulty is knowing what our blind spots are. One Sunday morning I was on my way to a church to preach. I was entering I-490 West on the left side from I-590 South in Rochester. I looked in my rearview mirror, saw nothing coming, and started to pull over into the next lane. Just then I heard a horn blowing furiously. I turned quickly back just in time to see a woman go whizzing by me. If looks could kill, I would not be here right now. She was very unhappy with me. Who could blame her? I was about to do a dumb thing that would have been endangered both of us. I want to be a safe driver and am most of the time. That day, I forgot about the blind spot between my peripheral vision and the area covered by the rearview mirror. I could see all around except at that one place. The danger was right at the very point where I could not see. I could hope as I continued on to church that my preaching would not be afflicted with a similar blind spot in the spiritual vision I brought to the pulpit.

The dangerous thing about having a blind spot is that you don't know you have it. We don't see something, but we don't know we are not seeing it. So we plunge confidently ahead. Grace here is truly a pure gift that we can only accept in gratitude without even knowing what God is forgiving us for. All we can do is to acknowledge the fact that we have blind spots and rejoice in the unmerited favor that sets us free from the despair we might otherwise feel once the certainty of certainty is dissolved. God saves us even from the bad things we do in complete ignorance and with the best of intentions.

The conclusion of the matter is that grace defines the framework of the Christian life in all its parts. It is the atmosphere in which we live and breathe. The love of God sets us free from anxious concern about our imperfect achievements without cancelling the obligation to do what is possible. The confidence that we are loved no matter what sets us free to be what we are and to do what we can. We act on the basis of the insight we do have. We trust God to forgive us for our blind spots as we proceed. Grace, grace, amazing grace!

Before we conclude, one more point has to be made. It is one thing that God loves us no matter what and another thing for us to believe it in our hearts. No matter if God is trustworthy, that fact is to no avail unless we deeply trust that trustworthiness. At this very point we confront one of the most slippery issues in all of Christian thought. Suffice it to say that the truth in the old doctrine of predestination is that not only are we saved by grace but that God enables us to make the response of faith by which grace is appropriated. God offers us the gift and makes possible our acceptance of it. The troubling fact is that some receive the gift to accept the gift and some don't. We can only hope that as we work out our salvation in fear and trembling, God will work successfully in us to evoke a responsive love and trust by which grace may become effective in our own lives. That miracle happens now and again but not always. It occurs, if it does, when in the dark wilderness of life a bush burns with sufficient glow and steadiness to evoke that wild leap of affirmation. That evocative flame enables us to believe that, despite all that appears to the contrary, at the heart of all things is an everlasting fire whose name is love.

The Consolations
Of Faith

Why Do We Suffer?

Job 1; Psalm 69

He died all alone in a little cabin far removed from his family. It was not the way anybody wanted it, but Uncle Volney had smallpox. It happened nearly 100 years ago. I heard the story from my grandmother. Volney Smith was her brother. The story of how he died while still quite a young man is one of those memories that connects me with the past. As Grandmother Martha Harris told it, people all around were dying, although some survived and took care of others. Uncle Volney was one of the unlucky ones. He was put off in a little cabin by himself. To reduce the danger of spreading the disease, his food was taken halfway from the kitchen to his cabin. He would come the rest of the way to get his meals when everyone had gone. One day he didn't come out. He died all alone, isolated from his family. Some men in the community who had survived the epidemic came to get his body. They put Uncle Volney in a wagon and took him to New Hope Baptist Church at midnight. They rang a bell all the way to warn those who had not had the disease to stay far away. They buried his body in the middle of the night. Once again he was alone in death as he had been at the end of his life.

The world is full of sad stories. Any week that passes will produce enough tragedy to keep the earth flooded with tears. Suffering goes on all around us all the time. During the past few days prior to my writing these words, the following stories have been in the news: A little five-year-old girl was snatched away from her mother in a public place and at last report had not been found. One moment she was there by her mother, the next minute she was gone. A family of four was brutally murdered in a nearby city not too long ago. They were attacked, tortured, and killed in their own homes by strangers who randomly chose their house. More than a dozen women in the Rochester, New York, area were murdered. Nearly all of them were involved in prostitution and connected with drugs. A young man went berserk in Canada and killed fourteen women on the campus of the University of Montreal. Having known much failure and rejection, he was full of hostility. He expressed it in one moment of violent madness that finally left him as well as his victims suddenly robbed of life. Terry Anderson was a captive of terrorists in Lebanon for many tears. We never know when we will hear of another shooting in a school. No more than five minutes after I had written the previous sentence on March 22, 2001, my wife called from downstairs to tell me that another school shooting had occurred.

A television show recently told the story of a young man in Chicago who had in desperation broken into the intensive care unit where his child was being kept alive by machines. He waved a gun to keep people away and pulled out the plugs. He held his son until he died. The child had swallowed a balloon and almost choked to death. His brain had been deprived of oxygen for a long time. He had no hope of ever being more than a vegetable. Doctors agreed that the infant would never be conscious again. The court refused permission to take away the technology that kept him breathing. The father out of love for the child and in desperation took extreme measures to relieve the suffering of all involved. Fortunately, a grand jury had the good sense not to indict him.

Seldom does a day pass but that we read newspaper accounts of people being killed or maimed by drunken drivers. A trial took place in Kentucky in which an intoxicated man ran into a bus and killed 27 people. Hardly a more heart-wrenching sight can be imagined than a mother full of agony and anger telling how her teenage daughter's life was taken in a crash caused by a driver stupid enough to drive a car while poisoned with alcohol. I can no longer laugh at impersonations of drunks with slurred speech. The list can be made as long as we want it to be. We have not mentioned the thousands of children at this moment dying of hunger, the homeless who roam the streets, the victims of cancer and AIDS and a hundred other diseases. There are the lonely, the despairing, the unloved, the unwanted, the mentally ill, all the rest of those who suffer from the manifold ills to which this frail flesh of ours is heir.

A few years ago one of the books that stayed high on the bestseller list for a long time was Rabbi Harold Kushner's *When Bad Things Happen to Good People*. That idea touches something deep in all of us. For who is there who has not at some time wondered about and agonized over the fact that bad things happen to good people? By good people we do not mean perfect people. There are none. We have in mind folks who by and large try to do the right thing, people who would not deliberately do anything cruel or harmful to other people. They have done much good in their lives. Suddenly the evil days come upon them. They are solid citizens whose hearts are usually in the right place and whose deeds testify to a kind of basic integrity. Why do such bad things happen to people like that?

By bad things we mean those terrible afflictions of body and spirit that make life miserable. Accidents, disease, and violent crime come upon us without our consent. Disease strikes randomly without warning. Babies are born with congenital defects. Things can be going well, when an accident suddenly maims and mangles us for life. On November 30, 1988, I began to have chest pains about 9 p.m. on a Wednesday night. I spent eight days in Strong Memorial Hospital and came out with a fresh sense of the frailty and mortality of human flesh. On May 13, 1997, my wife noticed symptoms that suggested that I might be having a stroke. I was and spent two weeks in the hospital. Fortunately, I have fully recovered from both events and am in splendid health. But who knows what might happen to me or to you within the next 24 hours?

We need not multiply examples. The fact and the mystery of suffering are all around us. Says Job in the midst of his misery, "I am not at ease; nor am I quiet; I have no rest; but trouble comes" (Job 1:26). Says the Psalmist, "I am weary with my crying; my throat is parched. My eyes grow dim with waiting for my God" (Psalm 69:3). These ancient cries are as modern as the computer on which I write these words. No fact of life raises more difficult problems for our Christian faith. How can so much pain and injustice exist in a world created by a God who is supposed to be perfectly good and all-powerful? In the classroom, we call it the problem of evil. We look to the Scriptures and to the great thinkers of the Church, past and present, for insight and understanding.[1]

I have struggled with this problem as long as I can remember. Yet my own life has been almost uninterruptedly good. My question most often is, "Lord, why have so many good things happened to me, when others have known such tragedy?" Oh, I have had my own heartache and struggle. On one occasion years ago life seemed dark and hopeless. I can recall a few hours in deep despair when I came to know in my own heart how people could get desperate enough to take their own lives. That episode of hopelessness pales, however, in the face of all the good years and all the success and happiness I have known.

Nevertheless, as a preacher and theologian, it is the problem of evil and suffering that has concerned me over the years. I do not wish to immerse you in the endless debates of the theologians and philosophers who have wrestled with Job's predicament. There is no simple answer or set of propositions that applies to all the miseries and injustices that plague the world. In the Bible many different things are said about suffering. Nowhere is there a systematic analysis of its sources or meaning. Life is complicated and multidimensional. Many things are true about our lives and our distress. What applies to some circumstances is not pertinent to others. Neither the Scriptures nor human reason gives us a satisfactory solution to all our questions.

I offer a few considerations that have been helpful in my own struggles. Let us proceed by looking at the world God has created and at our place in the world. In the first place, much of the suffering in the world is caused by what people do to each other. God has given us the power of choice. We bring a lot of misery on ourselves by our foolishness, our carelessness, and our selfishness. Murders, cruelty, crime, and all sorts of meanness and injustice are committed by people out of fear, hate, and greed. Drunken drivers who kill and maim are abusing their freedom, however much they may be suffering from a disease. We hurt ourselves, and people hurt each other by their acts, attitudes, and choices. We all, in varying degrees, dishonor the freedom which God has given us.

All this does not necessarily mean that a person could have done otherwise than he or she did at a given moment. Some people may be addicted to their bad habits and act out of compulsions over which they have little or no control. What we decide expresses what we are. If we develop an evil character, we will do evil deeds. Nevertheless, if we choose to do what hurts others, we are responsible, since we did it. We cannot hold God directly responsible for the misery which we cause by our own actions.

In the second place, the very nature of reality makes it inevitable that accidents, diseases, and destruction will sometimes occur. Look at it this way. Atoms, molecules, stones, trees, animals, and people all have parts arranged in a certain way that make them what they are. If this organization is disturbed, destruction occurs. This means everything is vulnerable, fragile, and subject to disruption. This is closely related to the fact that we live in an interdependent, law-abiding world. Things interact with good and bad effects. They may interfere with each other. Destruction may result. Accidents happen. Things collide, get broken, fall apart, blow up, erode, rust, and rot. If we are talking about living organisms, disorganization among their parts causes pain and eventually death. Suffering is a disturbance of healthy functioning in the body or mind of a living being. Human bodies get sick and die. They are mangled and destroyed by stones, bullets, storms, earthquakes, and other devastations too numerous to list. It may be that any real world worth living in will be like this. It is hard to conceive of free, interacting beings that are not vulnerable. We are flesh. We bleed, hurt, suffer, and die.

It would appear that there cannot be a world in which good things can happen without the possibility of bad things happening. We cannot have one without the other. The very principles and processes that produce pleasure and happiness when they work properly produce misery when things go wrong. Let me illustrate. The digestive system is constructed to give us satisfaction when we eat good food. It follows that we can get a stomach ache if something upsets normal functioning.

Moreover, the more good that is possible, the more suffering is possible. Worms and cats cannot experience the heights of happiness that people can. Neither can they know the depths of misery we do. The fact that human beings can experience meaning and purpose that give us happiness means that we can also experience despair and hopelessness that make life awful. The same capacities that make human enjoyment possible make possible human suffering. We cannot have one without the other.

Finally, notice that complicated things are easy to break down. Consider the human brain. The complexity of this system of cells and connections is mind-boggling. It is this intricate arrangement of tissue that makes possible thought, love, choice, and all that makes human life distinctive. Yet this same complexity makes it very vulnerable. So much more can go wrong with a brain than with a mountain.

Note then:

1. The very same processes that make possible health and happiness when things go right lead to suffering when things go wrong. We cannot have good without the possibility of evil.
2. The more complex an organism is,
    a. the more good it can experience,
    b. the greater evil it can suffer, and
    c. the more can go wrong.

It does not seem possible to escape these facts and connections in our world. They may apply to any world that God might create.

What is the conclusion of the matter? Some bad things happen because people make them happen to themselves and each other. Some bad things happen because it is in the very nature of our world that they can occur. We might save ourselves from a lot of grief if we simply accepted the fact that people and things are the immediate causes of misery. Hence, it is not true that God directly causes particular instances of suffering. God does not make specific evil things happen for some reason. If we ask whether God wills this or that instance of suffering in an immediate way, the answer must be "No." Some passages of Scripture teach otherwise, of course. I do not believe we ought to see things this way today.

God is ultimately responsible for the *possibility* of bad things happening, since God made the world. But God does not cause each instance of suffering for a particular purpose.

Rather when accident, disease, and violence bring great pain and misery to us, I believe that God's heart is broken like ours. God feels our pain and suffers our agony with us. Only if this is so can I believe that God is truly full of love and compassion. Yet in our sorrow God and we can make the best of it from now on to bring new life and enjoyment out of the broken pieces.

God uses every event, good and bad, as an opportunity to work in us and through us and in all things to bring the greatest possible happiness, joy, and love into being. In that fact we can trust. So believing we can try to attune our lives to that saving purpose, knowing that nothing can separate us from the love of God.

Yes, in one sense, Uncle Volney died all alone. In another sense, he was surrounded by the love of God and by the love of his family. Around him was the tender compassion of all those who wished more than anything else they could be with him to hold his body and to comfort his spirit when his life was slipping away. Uncle Volney suffered, but he did not suffer alone. In that realization there is comfort and hope.

---

1. The preceding paragraphs were originally published in *The Many Faces Of Evil*, CSS Publishing Co., Lima, Ohio, 1997, pp. 21-23. Used by permission.

Consolation In Suffering

Romans 8:28-39

I knew when I saw him coming that something was wrong. I didn't know the news was that bad. I was about fourteen years old at the time. I had a friend whose name was Alfred Graham. He was two or three years older than I, but we spent a lot of time together. Alfred's father bought a motorcycle. After a time, Alfred learned to ride it and actually gave me a lesson or two. I only rode it once by myself down the road about a half a mile and back. Soon tragedy struck. One Saturday, Alfred's father was doing some work around the house and needed some nails. He got on the motorcycle and rode into town to make the purchase. We all lived out in the country in those days. On the way back, he was in an accident that killed him instantly.

At that time, my mother, my father, and I had taken the job of cleaning the little country church where we were all members. That Saturday afternoon we were getting things ready for Sunday when Alfred came to tell us that his father had been killed. It was a very sad time. I shall never forget being in Alfred's house that weekend and hearing his mother crying out in her agony. Over and over, she screamed, "Why, why, why?" Those words sank deeply into my head and heart. I have often thought about those agonizing words as I pondered the question of suffering, accidents, and tragedy in the light of Christian faith.

In particular, I have wondered just what Alfred's mother meant by her question. What exactly was she asking? What kind of answer was she looking for? What could anyone have said that would have been a satisfactory reply? I don't know, of course, exactly what was in her mind. I have struggled with her question and with the various answers one might give. Nothing would have wiped away her sorrow. In one sense, she was not looking for anyone to take away her pain with some kind of intellectual response. It was, in part, simply a way of expressing her deep distress and anguish in the face of the unanswerable. Yet decades later her question still worries me. What can we say from this distance in the light of all that is involved?

At one level, a clear and simple answer is available. We know *why* it happened if why means how. Mr. Graham was coming down Hill Street at the edge of town. A truck was in front of him. He pulled over into the left lane to pass. As he began to pull around, the truck made a left turn. He ran into the back of the truck. His skull was split, killing him at once. I am sure that her question was not simply about the sequence of events that led up to the accident. Much more remains to be dealt with.

At another level, perhaps she was asking, "Why me? Why him? Why us? Why now, when thing are going so well? Why now, when we thought we had many more years together? Why, when he was in the prime of life with so much to live for?" We are in a much more difficult realm now. We are talking about meaning and purpose. We could, of course, say that accidents can happen to anyone. Tragedy is no respecter of persons. No guarantees are available for anybody. No security can be purchased that will preserve us from disaster. Things like that occur. They can happen to anyone at any time. No one of us knows what we may face before the day, or the week, or the year is over. When we read in the papers about some terrible thing, don't we frequently say to ourselves, "There, but for the grace of God, or there, but for good fortune, go I." We know deep down that it could happen to us; yet when it does happen, we cannot help but ask as Alfred's mother did, "Why?" We all knew that if Mr. Graham or the truck had for some reason been 45 seconds earlier or later in arriving at that very spot on Hill Street, it would not have happened. He and the truck were there in that crucial space at the same instant. Still we must press our question on a deeper level. "Why?"

There is a final level at which that question is raised. Here it has to do with the ultimate question of meaning and purpose in relationship to our faith in God. In this context, the question is whether God intended anything in what happened. Did God directly and immediately cause it for some reason? Did God arrange just that combination of circumstances, so that Mr. Graham and the truck would arrive at that precise moment? Was God responsible for the fact that the truck turned just as Alfred's father pulled around to pass?

I cannot believe that God directly and immediately causes things like this to happen. I take such a position with all humility and in fear and trembling. The mysteries of God are beyond our understanding. It would be the height of arrogance to say that I *know* what God does and does not do in particular cases. Beyond that I know that there are strong theological traditions which say otherwise. Many of us have been taught that every event which happens is under God's control. Nothing happens but that God intends it.

Contrary to that way of thinking, I have come through many years of struggle and thought to the conclusion that it is wrong to say that God directly and immediately causes every event to happen as it does. God is, of course, indirectly and ultimately responsible for what happens, since God created the world and determined how it would operate. Some distance, however, lies between God and the world. An intervening area must be recognized between God's general control over the world and the specific and particular things that actually happen. This intervening distance means that we have some freedom of action in which we determine what happens. By our own choices a chain of events is set off that sometimes results in good consequences and sometimes in catastrophe. In this arena we are free to learn and to grow. We must face the consequences of our choices. Sometimes we make mistakes and have to pay the cost.

Another area of action not immediately determined by the will of God can be located. In the world of nature is to be found a sort of independence in which things happen in accordance with laws, processes, and arrangements that God has built into the world. A set of events takes place that God does not directly cause. This means that it is wrong to think that God manipulates us like puppets on a string.

Why was Mr. Graham in an accident? He was in an accident because in working out his own purposes, he chose to go into town on an errand. He happened to be at that corner on Hill Street at a particular time. Meanwhile, the driver of the truck, carrying out his own purposes, happened to be there at the same time. As a result of these choices and actions, the collision occurred. The laws of nature held. Metal crashed into the tender tissues of a human body. Brains spilled onto the pavement in a sight that made one sick.

If God did not directly and immediately cause this accident, where was God in all of this? Was God involved at all? Yes, God was there in at least two ways. First of all God was present in sorrow and with a broken heart. God was there as the Suffering Companion who knows and cares, who feels every hurt and every grief of every creature. Jesus tells us that God has numbered the very hairs of our heads. Not a sparrow falls but that God takes notice.

God was present in a second way. God was there seeking to use that occasion as an opportunity to bring the greatest good out of that situation. God is present and at work in every event to increase happiness. God wants to bring about the most harmony, peace, and joy that can be had. Can we say how God does this? It might help to think about it this way. God has built into every living being an urge to fulfillment. The philosopher Whitehead said that in all life we find a three-fold drive: an urge to live, to live well, and to live better. God has implanted that motivation in us and in every living creature on the face of the earth. When something goes wrong, God is still there, working through that urge. God is present in that striving to bring the best out of the worst. In and through all events divine purpose redirects and remakes life. God wants whatever good is possible under changed circumstances to happen. God can use our tragedy and suffering as an opportunity to deepen our understanding of life and to strengthen our spiritual foundations.

A few years ago, I chanced to be watching a television program called *That's Incredible*. Usually one does not expect to learn much that is religiously important on a program like that. On this particular show, the story was told of a musician who had lost an arm to cancer. He was cast into great depression and despair. He played the saxophone, I believe. That was the way he made his living. His music was a source of great joy to him. All of that was lost. His life seemed to be in ruins. Then an electronic technician made a device that could be attached to the stump of his arm. By connecting this machine to the nerve endings on one end and to the instrument on the other end, it was possible for him to play again. After a lot of practice, he gained his old skill back. He was brought on the stage so that we could watch him get connected to this device. Then he played — beautifully. He obviously was a very happy man. It was as though he had come back from death to life. Then he spoke. His words were quite remarkable. He said, "I would not have my arm back even if I could. Back then, I did not know what life was all about. Since I lost my arm, I have learned so much. I am such a different person that I had rather be where I am now than where I was when I had my arm."

It would be wrong, I think, to say that God arranged things to make this man get cancer in his arm in order to learn these lessons about life. It would be more accurate to believe that the cancer was the result of something going wrong in his body. Surely, God would have preferred the deepening of his spiritual life to occur in a more normal and healthy way, without the loss of his arm. Surely, God was sorry that the pain and misery happened. Nevertheless, it seems completely in accordance with our faith in a loving, caring God to think that God was at work in the opportunity that his illness provided to bring him to a deeper understanding and appreciation of life and love.

How does God work to bring about the best that is possible? I do not pretend to understand all mysteries and to have all knowledge. I have thought about it a lot over many years. One thing can be said. God creates life with a built-in resurrection potential. I have already quoted Whitehead who taught that all creatures have an urge to live and to live well and to live better. Now something more can be said. That urge is so strong that when it is frustrated, it seeks ways to overcome obstacles and make the best of the situation. Life keeps coming back from defeat and rises up to try again. When one path is blocked, another is sought.

I didn't see the cartoon. A friend told me about it. It showed a little stick figure arranged to look like a person. Let us call this little person Human. Human was running around having a good time. Then a fist or something like it came down and crushed this little creature. Soon Human got up and started running again. A bigger fist came down and mashed Human right into the earth. This time it took a little longer. After a while Human struggled to get up and move once more. Well, you know how it went. The fist got bigger and bigger. The blow got heavier and more devastating. Every time Human came back. It took longer and longer. The feet were a little less steady. Nevertheless, life went on.

Finally, there was one last assault. A huge fist that overflowed the screen came down in a mighty force with a tremendous crashing noise. Human was crushed flat to the surface. All was quiet. No movement could be seen. Human, it appeared, was done for. It was all over. This last slam was too much. We watch. Nothing happens. Just when it appears that it is time to put up a little stone marking the place where the end came, a slight stirring can be seen. Then all is quiet again. After some time, another little commotion is evident. Slowly, gradually, painfully, Human struggles, falls, rises again, and at last stands unsteadily but surely. Then Human walks away.

I think this is what the cross and resurrection symbolize for human life on this earth. Life comes with a built-in resurrection potential that never ceases to look for a way to overcome and press on to victory.

What, then, is our consolation in the midst of tragedy and suffering? We can say at least two things. The first is that God suffers with us as the loving Companion who is always near, who always cares, who feels our hurts and knows our sorrows. The second thing to be said is that God never ceases to work in all things through the processes of nature and through our freedom to bring the greatest possible good out of every situation.

When tragedy and suffering come, we cannot help asking, "Why?" We can never fully answer that question. Life is full of meaning. Life is also full of mystery. We can be assured with some confidence that God is with us in all things. God gives us the gift of existence and builds into life an urge toward living to the fullest. God is with us to share all our sorrows and our joys. As the Creator, God makes use of every opportunity to bring good out of the potential with which we are born. As the Redeemer, God continues to work to bring new good out of evil, new life out of death, hope out of despair, and resurrection from every cross. Such consolation does not remove the heartache and pain. It does provide us with the courage to keep on living and trying, knowing that we are not alone.[1]

---

1. Most of this sermon was originally published in *The Many Faces Of Evil*, CSS Publishing Co., Lima, Ohio, 1997, pp. 121-128. Used by permission.

A Sermon For Saturday

Psalm 22; Matthew 27:46

What do you do when there is nothing more you can do? You have gone as far as possible, and still the dark night of the soul continues. You have tried everything, but the pain of the body persists. This is a difficult and delicate subject. The gospel is good news. Here I am about to suggest that sometimes the bad news prevails. Knowing that I cannot speak the whole truth and nothing but the truth, perhaps it would be better not even to suggest that times come when salvation is far away. Four points made quickly will help clarify what I am about.

1. No trick lurks in the question. Do not expect that in the last five seconds, I will attempt a 75-yard homiletical field goal and turn what looked like certain defeat into glorious triumph. I do not have a hidden theological rabbit that I will suddenly pull with rhetorical magic out of nowhere just in the nick of time. I do not propose at the end to say that despite everything there is actually one more thing you can do that will finally work. The last line of this sermon will not be "and they all lived happily ever after."

2. A sermon like this takes the risk of emphasizing the negative. We are commissioned to preach the gospel, to proclaim good news. Enough bad news we have already. Cynicism, doubt, despair abound. Hope is what we need. Really now, must we submit to the proposition that patches of darkness may come along that no light can penetrate? It is especially risky for a theological professor to tackle this problem. The word already is abroad that frequently we put too much lemon in the tea. Nevertheless, at least once in a lifetime, a chance must be taken to walk to the very edge

of realism even though one risks falling from the cliff into the abyss of despair.

3. A further risk is the danger of confirming our tendency to avoid responsibility. Sometimes when I say there is nothing more I can do, I could do something. But it is difficult, and I don't want to do it. I had rather enjoy my bad health than take the bitter medicine that is sitting on the shelf with the power to cure. The difference between "unable" and "unwilling" is not easy to figure out. At some point one slides into the other no matter which one you start with.

I have no desire to encourage escapism either in myself or in others. Nevertheless, I am going to be stubborn in my claim that sometimes "unable" really does mean that a given person has done all that he or she can do. Still the agony will not abate.

4. A final hazard is that we are prone to give up too soon. We have tried 98 different formulas. Still the iron has not turned to gold. We have read 47 books. Not one has offered an encouraging word. The skies are still cloudy all day. If at once you don't succeed, try, try again. Lo and behold, the ninety-ninth formula or the forty-eighth book may come up with something that works. Sometimes when we have tried psychiatry with no avail and have tried prayer with no answer, it may be that a little common sense insight and a little chicken soup will do the trick.

Yes, we often give up too soon. No sadder story has ever been told than that of the mountain hunter caught in a blinding blizzard. He gives up and dies in the darkness eight steps from the door of his warm and safe cabin. Oh, had he but tried just a little bit longer and stumbled just a few feet farther, he would have been saved after all. That is not the message of the day. In my story the storm is fierce, the night is dark, the wanderer is cold and exhausted. No living soul can be found anywhere. No warm cabin exists for miles around.

It should be clear by now that I intend to pursue my thesis all the way without blinking. My point is simply this: A Saturday comes between Good Friday and Easter Sunday. Sometimes that is where we find ourselves. The crucifixion lies in the past. The resurrection lies in the future and is but still a hope. The present moment is darkness and death.

I do not wish to deny that in the fullness of faith, we can rise in hopeful affirmation to join Paul in saying that we rejoice even in our sufferings. I do not wish to deny that suffering may produce endurance, and endurance may produce character, and character may produce hope that does not disappoint because God's love has been poured into our hearts through the Holy Spirit (Romans 5:1-5). I do wish to proclaim that suffering may produce exhaustion, and exhaustion destroys character. The loss of character produces despair, because hatred toward God is being poured into the heart by a cynical spirit toward life.

I do not wish to deny that Christian faith can rise to marvelous heights and face tribulation, distress, persecution, famine, nakedness, peril, and sword and conquer them all. I do not wish to deny that faith can conquer all in the assurance that neither death, nor life, nor angels, nor principalities, nor things present, nor things to come, nor powers, nor height, nor depths, nor anything else in all creation can separate us from the love of God in Christ Jesus our Lord (Romans 8:35-39). I do insist that it is not always so.

What do I do in those moments when I am being conquered in body by disease or in spirit by despair? What do I do when I am being separated from the love of God by circumstances far less threatening than famine or sword or far less capable of destruction than supernatural devils and demons?

We are reaching the crucial point. We are in the vicinity of the treasure of truth we are seeking. When I say I am unable to rejoice in my suffering, the descendants of the friends of Job gather round. They have an answer. When I say I am being less than a conqueror and that I am separated from the love of God, priests and preachers, theologians and therapists, point their fingers at me. They have a solution. I listen to their answers. I receive their solutions. At last perhaps I can be free from my burden and, like them, know how to slay the dragons. As the answers come in from the friends of Job and as the solutions pour forth from priests and preachers, from theologians and therapists, frequently are heard two discouraging words. My face gets cloudy for the rest of the day. Just when I thought I was going to find out what I could do in my distress, I heard those two words. Again and again, I heard them. Those who said them seemed not to notice that these two little words are the most important of all. You can rejoice in your sufferings, *if only* you get right with God. You can experience the love of God, *if only* you will believe. You can be healed, *if only* you have faith. You can be free from your guilt, *if only* you will accept your acceptance. You can overcome your depression, *if only* you will express your buried anger. You can be saved, *if only* you will accept the Lord Jesus as your personal Savior. You can have the gift of grace, *if only* you will receive it. Yes, you can do anything, *if only*. That's what I hear from the friends of Job, from the theologians and the therapists, from the preachers and the priests.

Wait, I say! Stop! Back up! Come again, once more, slowly, with your answers and your solutions. This time, tell me how I do all those things that come after those two little words, *if only*. Don't you see, that's my problem. *If* I could do all those things, *if* I could believe, trust, accept, receive, get angry, etc., etc., etc., my predicament would be a lot less serious than it is.

More than three decades ago I was involved in some group therapy. After a few sessions, some members of the group told me they were unable to be of much help to me. I was not expressing any deep feelings. All they got from me were words that came from the top of my head and not feelings from deep in the gut. They were right. Here were those two words again. *If only* I would pour out my feelings to them, we could make some progress. My response was that *if* I were free and spontaneous with my feelings, *if* I could get in touch with my buried anger, *if* I could vomit up the garbage in my guts, then, of course, we could move ahead. I don't seem to be able to. That's my problem. Can you help me with that? Can you help me do what comes after the "*if only*"? It may be that I was not unable to get in touch with my feelings but just unwilling. Nevertheless, I seemed stuck.

When I was a child, I was told that I could catch a bird. All I had to do was sprinkle salt on its tail. Wow, I thought! I can catch birds in my hand. There was just one little problem. Every time I slipped up on a mockingbird to perform the magic ritual, the little critter flew away. I was left standing there on one foot like a fool, salt shaker poised in mid-air. I could catch birds, *if only* I could get close enough. Yes, you too can catch birds today by just sprinkling salt on their tails. Don't ask me how you can keep them from flying away before you get close enough with the salt. You will have to figure out the details for yourself.

Yes, there is a Saturday between Good Friday and Easter Sunday. Sometimes some of us find ourselves between crucifixion and resurrection. My hero today is the author of Psalm 22. This agonized soul knew what living on Saturday is like. "My God, my God, why hast thou forsaken me?" It was these words that Jesus uttered from the cross just before he died. Frequently, exegetes feel a need to explain these words away. Jesus must not be allowed to utter those awful thoughts. Surely Jesus did not feel forsaken by the Almighty even in this hour of extremity. No, Jesus must have a faith unmarred even by temporary doubt.

So the experts rush in to remind us that Jesus was beginning to quote Psalm 22. While it begins with estrangement, it ends on a note of praise. Supposedly I should feel better knowing that had Jesus quoted the whole Psalm, the sting of his opening words would be modified. Somehow I do not feel better. Something in me wants to side with those interpreters who speak of this cry of dereliction as expressing a genuine sense of loneliness and despair. For in those dark moments of the soul, these awful words from the cross provide the point at which we can most fully identify with Jesus.

I do not feel comfortable when I hear Jesus urging me to love my enemies. I have difficulty enough putting up with my friends. I am threatened when I take seriously his words about taking up the cross. I am alienated by the command to go the second mile with the oppressor. I don't even want to go the first mile. This Jesus lays on me more than I can bear. I would like to live the life of a comfortable middle-class professional. All these radical demands about selling all, giving all, forsaking everything and following him, loving neighbors equally with myself, keep threatening to break into all the nice little compromises and rationalizations with which I defend my affluence and privilege and soft living.

Yet when Jesus seems most vulnerable and to be touched with the dread of ultimate despair that unites him most with the rest of us, some of the experts would take it away. They would have us believe that Jesus didn't really mean it. Surely, they say, he did not really feel forsaken after all. Yet it is from Jesus that we get the imagery of the Saturday of death before the resurrected life of Easter Sunday. It is from this very Jesus who in his utmost extremity at the point of disgraceful death cried out, "My God, my God why hast thou forsaken me?"

So I repeat, my hero for this hour is the author of the Psalm itself. This unknown soul can find no relief even though praying earnestly for mercy and healing. The agony of body and spirit is immense. No relief is in sight. Two things stand out.

First, our author remembers times in the past when God's goodness and saving power were manifest. Reference is made to the Psalmist's ancestors who trusted God and were delivered from their distress. There is also mention of the author's own early life. "Yet thou art he who took me from my mother's womb; thou didst keep me safe upon my mother's breast" (Psalm 22:9).

Secondly, the Psalmist promises that if God will bring relief now, a service of public praise will be held. Gratitude to God will be offered. God's goodness and mercy will be extolled. A hymn glorifying God will be sung. This hymn promises future generations that God can be counted on. Posterity will serve God and continue to proclaim deliverance to generations yet unborn.

What happened to this poor soul we do not know. Maybe the suffering wretch died in misery and without relief. Even in the midst of unabated pain, alienation, and abandonment, the Psalmist remembers past mercies to God's people, begs earnestly for a present renewal of those mercies, and promises to praise and serve God in the future if deliverance finally comes. If this unknown fellow sufferer can do this much in this midst of burdens far heavier than most of us bear, surely we can do no less.

Unless you think that despite everything I have tried to give a happy ending to the story, let me remind you that as the sermon comes to a close it is still Saturday. The author of Psalm 22 is still crying out, "My God, my God, why hast thou forsaken me?"

The Cross-Shaped Scar In The Heart Of God

Genesis 6:5-8; 9:12-15

The words stabbed me in the heart. They come back to me again and again. It was more than twenty years ago. I sat in the Detroit airport with a couple of hours to wait before my plane for Rochester departed. I bought a newspaper to pass the time. In an advice column I came across this letter:

> *Dear Jane Lee: I am an adult who was, and still am, despised and ridiculed because I am ugly ... I have a rock bottom opinion of myself. I've never had a friend. In school, my classmates used to torment me with their cruelties ... When I went to work, I was harassed by cruel taunts ... My husband doesn't have any feeling for me. He would have left long ago if he could have afforded it. He said once — at a time when I was pregnant with one of our children — that my face turns his stomach. I sure would like to earn some money to get an education and some of the nice things in life, but I am afraid to go any place because people stare or snicker ... I've never murdered anyone. I don't peddle drugs to the young. I've never stolen from others or slandered others. I do the best I can as a wife and mother ... I would have given up on life a long time ago, but somehow I keep looking for a rainbow.*[1]

What do we have to say as Christians to this poor soul who has suffered all her life because she is ugly? Our first response may be to assign responsibility to her for the way she reacts to the face she was born with. Maybe we want to admonish her sternly to stop wallowing in self-pity and do something about the situation. We quote that cute little platitude: If life deals you a lemon, make lemonade. Well, okay, but is that all we have to say? Do we hint that there must be some purpose in it, since God works for good in all things for those who believe (Romans 8:28)? Do we even suggest that suffering can be good for us, that it develops the soul? Do we quote again from Romans and urge her to rejoice in her suffering, since suffering leads through endurance to character and from character to hope (Romans 5:1-5)? Do we urge her to believe that God's grace is sufficient for every need? Beyond that, of course, in our psychologically-oriented age, we might urge her to seek a secular doctor of the soul. Surely what she finally needs is a psychotherapist. But is that the end of it?

I do not want to rule out any of these responses. They all may have a point. Nevertheless, if this is all that can be said, I am a bit uneasy. All that has been said so far puts the responsibility back on the shoulders of that poor woman. We have said that if she will only get right with God and have enough faith, if only she will have the right attitude about it, see it in the proper light, come to terms with the facts, take charge of her life, lemons can become lemonade.

And we seem so eager to get God off the hook. Either God has a purpose in it or will supply the grace that overcomes all. Or we are content to appeal to the mystery of God's ways of dealing with us. The assumption seems to be that the problem is finally all with her and not all with the fact that she was born ugly. No, we say, the difficulty lies with all those people who have treated her terribly. That is not God's fault. Maybe, but what accounts for the fact that she was born ugly? But, we protest, ugly is a subjective judgment, a cultural matter. God is not to blame for that. Maybe, but we all have some notion in our heads about who is beautiful and who is not even if we act nicely toward everybody. No matter how long this sort of conversation goes on, I am left troubled.

I want to pursue another line of thought. With heaviness of heart, I conclude that some suffering occurs that neither God nor the victims can fully overcome no matter how hard they struggle.

We are limited in the extent to which we can triumph over evil either in fact or in our spirits. God too is limited and labors to overcome evil with only partial success.

I revolt against the old Calvinist doctrine of predestination. The thought that God has chosen from all eternity some people to be saved and some to be damned forever is getting close to the most horrible idea conceivable. Let us hope it is not true. Nevertheless, a remnant of truth may be contained in a reinterpreted version. It does appear that some people in this life are born to be damned in some if not all aspects of their lives. I mean that they suffer as the victim of circumstances or the actions of others over which they have no control.

Rita Hayworth was beautiful and glamorous in the movies. She will be remembered as the most famous pin-up of World War II. It is an image that all of us old enough to remember have in our minds. She was married to some of the world's richest and most celebrated men. Yet the heading of the review in *The New York Times* reads: "What we have here is a very sad story." She was sexually abused by her father and exploited by him in terrible ways. At age twelve she sat fat and silent on her front porch staring straight ahead, afraid to play with other children. She lived through a lifetime of disastrous relationships and was manipulated and used by a succession of men. Her life deteriorated rapidly, punctuated by drinking sprees, irrational outbursts, and failing health. Her career disintegrated. At long last at age 62, she was diagnosed as being in an advanced stage of Alzheimer's disease. One redeeming note is that her daughter Yasmin became her legal guardian and took loving care of her until she died in 1987. I do not know all that is involved or how her own free will entered into the situation. It does appear that from early childhood on she was destroyed by powers over which she had limited control. She appears to have been damned from the start.

Listen to the stories of runaway children, of serial killers, of drug addicts and prostitutes. Look into the sad faces of starving babies in Africa. Consider the circumstances of those who populate the mental hospitals of the land for a lifetime, perpetually tormented in body and spirit. Hear the life histories of the homeless and destitute, those serving life sentences in prison. Whatever responsibility they have for their own destinies, I cannot escape the conclusion that an element of tragedy pervades it all. All around are people caught up, tossed about, mangled, and destroyed by forces over which they have limited control. One thirteen-year-old girl who had run away reported that she left home because her step-brother had raped her. Her father told her he was going to have her raped anyway. In all this is an element of the tragic — suffering that the victims could not totally prevent, nor can they always or fully overcome it. Neither is it always possible for them to triumph spiritually over all adversity by the resources of divine grace. They are damned in body and spirit.

Let me stress again that I do not want to ignore or even to underplay the role that human beings themselves play in determining their destiny. Is anyone so molded by circumstances that he or she could not have altered the outcome in any shape, form, or fashion? I doubt it. We usually have a choice within some range of available options. Of course, we do. Nor do I want to deny that some people do prevail spiritually over great obstacles. All I insist on is that there are limits to what we can do to prevent or to overcome the injustices, miseries, and calamities that beset us. What about that other part that determines our lives over which we have no control? However free we are, we are not unrestrictedly free to do anything we choose. We are free, but circumstances also create a destiny that we live out. It is in that portion of life beyond the range of human decision to alter that tragedy resides.

Have you ever watched the weight lifters compete during the Olympics? Here are athletes who have trained long and hard to develop their strength to the highest degree possible. The time has come. They bend and lift. Every muscle strains and trembles. They sweat and groan. They push their bodies until they have exhausted their powers. No matter how much they lift, they always reach a limit beyond which they simply cannot go. The weight comes crashing down. This is my point about life. We don't always exert ourselves to the extreme frontier of our creative capacity to make the lemons of our lives into lemonade. That's true. Sometimes we do not conquer the demons that torment us because we give up too soon or don't try hard enough. Until we pass that line between unwilling and unable, the limit we cannot exceed, the terrible has not yet become the tragic. But some human suffering lies beyond the region over which we have control. At that point, we are in the hands of powers that flesh and blood cannot conquer.[2]

It is one thing, however, to admit our own limits of strength, will, and imagination. It is quite another to concede that God has limits too. Christian tradition has said with a near unanimous voice that God is omnipotent. This God knows no bounds except those imposed by self-contradiction. God cannot make a short, straight stick with only one end, and the like. However, God can create worlds, control the winds and the seas, and raise the dead. Much in the Bible supports this view of God the Almighty. Yet here and there are hints of another view of God. Now and then we get a glimpse of a God who is caught up in conflict, struggle, pain, and bewilderment. This is the God who faces agonizing situations and who comes up against limits just as we do. This view is mostly neglected. I want to explore it here. Let me begin with one of the most familiar stories in the Bible. In Genesis 1 God looks at the freshly-made world and declares it to be very good. Only a few chapters later, things are not going so well. In fact, they are awful. The world is full of wrongdoing. The wickedness of humanity is massive. The imagination of people is on evil continually. Things are so bad that God regrets having created it all in the first place. The Creator is grieved. God said, "I am sorry I made the world and the people who live in it. They have made a terrible mess of the beautiful universe I put them in." God gets angry and decides to blot humanity from the face of the earth.

Look at how God is pictured in this passage. It is hard to imagine that this God is the omnipotent, omniscient, immutable, all-determining Will of Christian tradition. Genesis 6 offers us a God who is perplexed, angry, and deeply grieved. You get the impression that God is surprised, that this outcome was unforeseen and unexpected. Moreover, God is faced with agonizing alternatives. What a far cry from the God of orthodoxy! The God of tradition knows in advance everything that is to happen, has no emotions, confronts no unanticipated developments. The God who is sorry for having made the world is not the God who knew from the start that this would happen. So we have a picture of a God facing limits and having to grapple with some tough choices.

If I am not misreading this text, it appears that God is up against a frustrating situation. To blot out everything would destroy the purpose God had in mind in creating living beings to begin with. Yet the situation is so bad that it requires drastic action. So God decides to wipe out most life but to spare enough people and animals to make a fresh start. Noah, a good man, is given instructions to make an ark and gather representatives of every species of animal life into safety so that they can replenish the earth.

Marc Gellman has written a book of stories about stories in the Bible under the title *Does God Have A Big Toe?*[3] According to Gellman, when it is time for Noah to shut the door of the ark, some friends of his come dressed up in zebra suits asking to be let in. Noah has to refuse them, knowing they will drown. Noah is sad about this and is filled with tears. Finally, he says to his friends, "I love you. I am sorry for you, sorry for the animals, sorry for me, and sorry for God." Noah recognizes that this is a tragic situation that catches up everybody, including God. When the waters came and flooded the earth and killed all the people and all living things not on the ark, some said it was rain that fell. Others thought it surely must be the tears of God.

Later on, God rescues Israel from the armies of Pharaoh but in doing so ends up killing Egyptians in the Red Sea. God loves them too. Just before that, God's efforts to free Israel had resulted in the death of every firstborn son in every Hebrew family. Centuries later when God sent the Messiah, one consequence was that every male in the vicinity of Bethlehem under two years of age was killed at the instigation of Herod. How it must have pained God to know that because of Moses and now Jesus all those homes were filled with terror and sorrow without measure.

I cannot claim that the Bible as a whole supports me. Nevertheless, reflection on Scripture and experience has led me against my will to a doctrine of a finite, suffering, struggling God. God, I believe, has a hard time too. There are limits to what God can accomplish on earth. Because God loves, God agonizes with the world and with all human beings in their torment. The only God I can believe in is a God with a broken heart, a God who weeps, our companion and support. God is the Fellow-Sufferer who shares our grief, who feels the pain of our sorrows.

I don't know what happened to that woman who lived a dreadful life because she was ugly. I wonder whether she finally gave up or whether she found the rainbow she was looking for. After everything else is said, I want to say to her that God knows, and God cares. I want to say that God did not make you ugly for some hidden divine purpose. I believe that the reason you were born ugly is not because God intended it but because God could not prevent it. But God suffers with you in your agony. God shares your pain as one who has a hard time too. God has a heart with a scar in the shape of a cross. That heart is broken for you.[4]

God must have been tempted in the time of Noah to give up upon seeing the sorry state to which the world had come. Yet God looked for a way out and used the rainbow as a pledge not to quit the struggle. I hope that woman I read about in the Detroit airport many years ago kept on trying too. I hope she found her rainbow. Maybe the rains are the tears of God still falling for her and for all who suffer the threats and terrors of this life.

---

1. *The Detroit News*, October 14, 1976.

2. The preceding paragraphs were originally published in *The Many Faces Of Evil*, CSS Publishing Co., Lima, Ohio, 1997, pp. 95-99. Used by permission.

3. Marc Gellman, *Does God Have A Big Toe?* (New York: HarperCollins Children's Books, 1993).

4. The preceding paragraph was originally published in *The Many Faces Of Evil*, CSS Publishing Co., Lima, Ohio, 1997, p. 101. Used by permission.

Living In A
Complicated World

Is It Any Fun Being Good?

Psalm 1; Romans 12:9-21

An underground current in our thinking has it that being good is no fun at all. This idea usually comes out in a humorous way. Perhaps we don't want to admit that we share the belief. So we tell a joke. The point is made. The tension is relieved. And we go on about our business. Our sense of what we ought to believe is preserved. We never quite say right out loud that morality is a grievous burden. Let me give some examples of how we make the point with humor.

> *A cartoon in a magazine shows two men being led down into hell. One of them says to the other, "I envy you. Mine were all sins of omission." Poor guy. What a tragedy. Here he is on his way to hell, and yet he missed out on all the good times he could have had with all those sins of commission!*

> *Another cartoon shows Moses on the mountain receiving tablets of stone with the ten commandments on them. Moses says to God, "Couldn't you give them to us one at a time?" The point is obvious. Morality is hard and burdensome. Wouldn't it be nice to tiptoe into the laws of God and not have to face the whole set at once?*

> *Ty Ty, the old man in Ernest Caldwell's novel God's Little Acre, put it this way. "Coffee is so good, I don't understand why it's not a sin to drink it." We smile when we hear that because deep in us is a suspicion that if*

we really enjoy something, if it really feels good, it must be bad. How long has it been since you heard someone say, "Everything I like to do is either illegal, immoral, or fattening"?

The very day I was writing this, I got another illustration from the comic strips. Hagar the Horrible is sitting down to eat. He points to the plate in front of him and asks, "What's this?" His wife says, "Eat it; it's good for you." Hagar replies, " 'Eat it, it's good for you' is my least favorite dish."

Finally, you all know the story of the teenage girl who is leaving for a date. Her mother says, "Be good. Have a good time." The girl answers, "Well, make up your mind. Which is it?" Somehow "being good" and "having a good time" don't seem quite to fit each other.

We could multiply the examples. We all recognize that floating around in our heads is the notion that fun, pleasure, and enjoyment are bad or at least bad for you. Morality, duty, and righteousness are burdensome, a drag. A partial explanation may be that a bit of what we caricature as Puritanism still informs our mental outlook. I believe it was H. L. Mencken who defined Puritanism as "the fear that somebody, somewhere, is having a good time." It is still hard for us even today to associate having a good time with living up to the highest moral standards. In a special way, we have associated sex with naughtiness or even badness. Or at least we suspect that it might be more fun if morality did not put restrictions on its enjoyment. That may be changing a little bit. Now some of us older people say, "I can remember when the air was clean and sex was dirty." We associate other indulgences of the flesh with the good life. It is common for someone to say, "People who don't drink, smoke, gamble, or overeat don't really live longer. It just seems longer."

If we dwell only on the idea that morality and the pleasures of the body don't mix, we will miss the deeper dimension of the problem. We also have in our minds the notion that righteousness and duty are strenuous, difficult, and self-denying. We have a sense that what we ought to do and what we naturally want to do are in conflict. And well we might think this way. Consider what Jesus said about the way of salvation. When the lawyer said that the greatest commandments were to love God with all your being and your neighbor as yourself, Jesus agreed and said, "Do this and live." In the Sermon on the Mount, he defined the righteousness of the kingdom in even more demanding terms. Go the second mile. Love your enemy. Go the second mile voluntarily with the obnoxious Roman soldier who compels you to carry his things the first mile? Love your enemies — those who would destroy you if they could? Consider your neighbor's good equal to your own? Be as concerned that your neighbor's children get a college education as you are dedicated to your own children? If that is what is required of us, surely the law of God is a burden. Righteousness and love do not seem to define the good life, if that is what is required of us. Where is the good news in all that?

The problem is stated eloquently in Plato's *Republic*. Socrates is trying to define justice and to defend it as being identical with the best life possible. Glaucon makes the opposite case. He argues that people naturally prefer doing injustice to doing justice. People agree to live justly with each other as a compromise between the best life, which is to do injustice without being punished, and the worst life, which is to suffer injustice without having the power to retaliate.

Glaucon went on to illustrate his point by telling the story of Gyges's ring. Suppose there were a magic ring that would make you invisible if you turned it around on your finger. Just think what you could do if you had this ring. You could go into stores and take whatever you wanted. You could seduce your neighbor's spouse. You could listen in on any conversation you wanted to. You could go wherever you wanted to and do whatever you chose. You could live like a god! Now suppose there were only two of these magic rings. Let us give one to a just person and the other to an unjust person. If we observe them, sooner or later we will see them doing exactly the same things. Since the benefits are so great, would not everybody with such a magic ring end up living the unjust life?

Glaucon ended his argument with the proposal that the very best life would be to live unjustly but to have the reputation of being just. The worst life would be to live justly but to have the reputation of being unjust.

Adiemantus jumped into the fray. More remains to be said. The universal voice of humankind is that justice and virtue are honorable but grievous and toilsome. Pleasure and vice are easy and to be preferred. Well, Socrates, what do you have to say to all this?

Socrates admits that the challenge is formidable. To answer will require a serious and lengthy inquiry. You will be pleased to know that the details of the argument will not be repeated here. What it comes down to is this: Socrates builds his case on the proposition that justice in the soul is like health in the body. Justice, whether in the individual or in society, is present when all the parts of the organism work together, each doing its own proper task in concert with all the rest. Justice is a state of health, harmony, integrity, unity, and wholeness. It is like a finely tuned musical instrument. Each string and each note contribute to the pleasing effect of the whole. Health is excellence of functioning in the body. Justice is excellence of functioning in the individual soul and in society.

That is the heart of the defense Socrates makes of the proposition that justice is to be preferred to injustice. I offer it as the strongest case that can be made. We do not always live that way. But deep inside we know that health is intrinsically good and to be preferred to sickness and disease. Surely that is what we must say to the skeptics in our time. And that is what we must say to the skeptical part of our own minds that laughs at the jokes and the cartoons that suggest that being good is no fun at all.

Certainly the Psalmist seems to agree with Socrates that righteousness is the health of the soul. Living in accordance with God's law is joy and happiness. "Blessed is the man (the person) who walks not in the counsel of the wicked, nor stands in the way of sinners, nor sits in the seat of scoffers; but ... takes delight in the Law of the Lord" (Psalm 1:1). Such a person is like a tree planted by streams of water that yields fruit in its season. The righteous person is like a healthy tree that prospers and produces fruit pleasant to the eye and good to eat.

If Socrates and the Psalmist and we agree that virtue is to the soul what physical health is to the body, why do we laugh at those jokes? Surely health is to be preferred to sickness. If righteousness is the life of harmony, wholeness, and excellence, and if that kind of life is intrinsically good, why do we find those cartoons funny?

Let me make some suggestions that search for the conflicts in our thinking and living. Remember that in the background is the assumption that humor is the way we deal with our divided minds. The first possibility has already been mentioned. It may be that in some of us there are still remnants of the view that pleasure and enjoyment are morally suspect. If that is the case, we need to move into a better understanding of a biblical way of thinking in which life is to be enjoyed to the fullest. Life should be robust, zestful, full of joy, involving all the senses and including the pleasures of the body. The only constraints are health and justice. The only restriction is that we do no harm to ourselves or others. The only prohibition is that we do not exalt ourselves at the expense of others. Our pleasures must not deny others equal or just access to the same opportunities.

The villains are selfishness and excess. Selfishness is the pursuit of our own ends that denies the rights and claims of others. And there is always the temptation to exceed healthy boundaries. Mae West once said, "Too much of a good thing is *wonderful*." We are always in danger of falling into that error. When things get out of hand, the quest for this world's pleasures becomes sensuality, gluttony, inordinate love of luxury, ease, and comfort. The good life requires restraint, moderation, a capacity for denying some immediate gratifications for the sake of our own well-being and the needs of others. I want more chocolate cake than would be good for my body. So the tension that sometimes becomes a contradiction lives within. We want enjoyment, but we resist discipline. We want pleasure, but we resist self-restraint. We relieve the tension in laughter.

The recognition that health and justice require effort and discipline already takes us into a second level. Health of body and soul is intrinsically good. It is to be preferred to illness and injustice. Yet the plain fact is that doing one's moral duty requires activity, energy, time, and sometimes blood, sweat, and tears. George Bernard Shaw once said that he got his exercise by being a pallbearer for his friends who took exercise. Well, George, that is a good line, but it is mostly nonsense. A healthy body requires vigorous, regular, proper activity that uses the muscles of the body. My doctor tells me that to keep my heart healthy I should work out on my "NordicTrack" for at least thirty minutes every other day with my pulse rate in my training zone. Some days I am tempted to skip.

With regard to meeting the needs of our neighbors, it is easier to center our concern on ourselves than it is to bear the burdens of others. Who wants to worry about starving children, the homeless, and victims of AIDS? Why can't the poor just go away or at least keep out of sight and let us go about our business? The moral demands of Jesus are strenuous indeed. He requires that we clothe the naked, feed the hungry, visit those in prison, heal the sick, and comfort the afflicted. He requires us to see to it that the poor and the outcasts get justice and relief. He urges us to love the unlovely and to take into account the needs of our enemies. It is summed up in the requirement that we regard our neighbor's need as equal to our own. The moral life is in some sense like climbing a steep mountain over a rough trail. The selfish life is like sliding downhill over smooth terrain. Loving others makes demands on us. This is where the basic contradiction arises.

We just seem naturally to prefer our good to the good of others. The Church has been nearly unanimous over the centuries in defining sin as loving ourselves too much and our neighbors too little. The basic fault is prideful exaltation of our own interests above the just claims of others. A conflict exists between what we naturally want to do and what ethically we should do. And we make jokes to relieve the tension.

This brings us to the third and final point. As long as any selfishness remains in us, loving our neighbor equally with ourselves will be a grievous burden. The more life is lived in tune with God and with our deepest nature, the less conflict there will be between what we want to do and what we ought to do. What, then, is required before we can take delight in the law of the Lord? The word of Jesus is clear. You must be born again. Only radical conversion from preoccupation with self to equal regard for neighbor can obliterate the gap between duty and desire. Only an inner transformation from prideful exaltation of self to loving God with the whole heart can erase the line between ought to and want to.

In recent years feminist theologians have insisted that this way of putting it is one-sided. It reflects a point of view that pertains to men more than to women. It applies to whose who have much power more than to those who have little. Here we have to refer again to Socrates. Health is balance, harmony, unity — neither too much nor too little. Those, whether men or women, whose sin is self-abnegation, self-depreciation, and lack of self-esteem also are in need of conversion. Transformation will be away from subservience, timidity, and passivity toward healthy self-affirmation. It will involve living out the claim to equality in every sphere of life in church and society.

In any case, whether our sin is that we love ourselves too much or too little, those who live in love and in balanced harmony with their neighbors can truly take delight in the law of the Lord. Happy is the person who does what is right, whose life is in tune with God. Blessed are those who do what is right as a good tree produces good fruit.

All this brings us to a surprising conclusion. Only the saints find that doing good is a lot of fun. And that is no joke!

Living With The Weeds In The Wheat

Matthew 13:24-30

Life is a mixture of good and evil. Experience and observation keep that fact before us. Philosophers speculate about this common knowledge. Could God have made a better world? Could God have created a world with more happiness and less misery? You will be relieved to know that I do not propose to pursue these debates. I will report a distinction between the optimist and the pessimist. The optimist believes this is the best of all possible worlds. The pessimist is afraid the optimist is right.

The Bible contains no arguments about possible worlds that God might have made. It does recognize that this actual world is full of trouble. Only in the Garden of Eden at the beginning and in the New Jerusalem at the end is life an unmixed blessing. In the course of history itself, paradise has been lost. Heaven is still a hope. Jesus told a simple story that illustrates the point. A farmer sowed good seed in his field. His enemy came by night and planted weeds among the wheat. Soon both were growing up together. The offending weed is apparently darnel, a grain that resembles wheat but is poisonous to eat. Shall an attempt be made to pull out the weeds? No, says the farmer, let them grow together until the harvest. Then a separation can be made. To pull up the weeds now would uproot some of the wheat as well. Perplexing problems arise with regard to the original meaning and literary history of this parable. It has been given varying interpretations over the centuries. I want to reflect on the meaning of life here and now that this story evokes in me.

In the first place, this story has meaning for our individual lives. Good and evil entwine themselves in our personal histories in unpredictable, unavoidable, and perplexing ways. Accidents and disease may overtake us. A downturn in the economy may take our jobs. The outbreak of war may send our children into combat. On the streets we are at the mercy of maniacs, criminals, drunken drivers, and next-door neighbors. A hurricane or tornado may destroy our property. An earthquake may shake down our homes. In a thousand ways life can be disrupted by forces beyond our control as well as by our foolish choices. The sinful and the tragic are interwoven in the fabric of our daily existence.

Lawrence Ferlinghetti has put it well in one of his poems appearing in *A Coney Island Of The Mind*. The point is that life is wonderful except for all the bad things that happen in the midst of all our happiness and fun. After listing a bunch of things that are particularly nice, he ends abruptly:

> Yes
>   but then right in the middle of it
>   comes the smiling
>   mortician.[1]

Such are the days of our lives as the world turns; life can be beautiful, but all of a sudden we are face-to-face with the undertaker.

In the second place, the parable tells us something about the inevitable compromises and trade-offs that accompany all our efforts to improve society. Here again the wheat and the weeds are closely bound up with each other. It is impossible to root out all evil and preserve only what is good. Illustrations abound. Soon another effort will be made in Congress to lower the tax on capital gains. Some argue that it is just another undeserved break for the rich. The rest of us will not benefit. Others contend that lowering the tax will raise incentives, spur investment in new enterprises, and generally do a lot a good for everybody. Recently the question of the minimum wage has been a matter of controversy. One side maintains that it will improve the lot of entry level workers who cannot support themselves or a family on the present wage rates that many people get stuck in these days. The other side argues that the consequence of raising wages by law will be a loss of employment for a significant number of people. As business people find themselves unable to compete when their labor costs are raised beyond what the market will bear, they will fire workers. Well, who is right in these arguments? It may be that both sides have some of the truth but that neither has the whole truth. Neither side may have as much truth as it claims for its position. We can readily see how self-interest, whether economic or political, corrupts principles. Yet the contending parties cover all this up by giving their arguments a halo of pure moral idealism they do not deserve.

My wife was a chaplain in Pennsylvania when a young man was brought into the emergency room badly burned in a motorcycle accident. He was in great torment and agony. He had no chance of survival. Despite all doctors could do, his condition was horrendous. He remained conscious. He wanted to die. His family stood helplessly by watching him suffer and slowly slip away. Should he be put out of his misery? It would seem to be an act of mercy for somebody who would and did die in a matter of days. Yet deliberately to kill someone is against the law and offends the conscience. We have a term that puts the dilemma before us — mercy killing. The moral law tells us to be merciful, but it forbids us to kill. What shall we do? Once again, weeds are growing in the wheat.

We have not even raised a question about the trade-off between unemployment and inflation. We have not touched upon whether private schools that practice segregation on religious grounds should be given a tax exemption. Not yet in the picture is whether the KKK should be allowed to march in Skokie, Illinois, where many survivors of Hitler's concentration camps live. We could go on forever, I suppose. The point is that in our social life as well as in our personal existence, wheat and weeds grow together. We have not much hope of reaching a state of perfection on earth in which that would not be the case.

In the third place, this simple story may also have implications for God's own involvement in the world. A story in the Jewish tradition makes the point powerfully. When the ministering angels saw the Egyptians floundering in the sea after the Israelites had passed over, they burst into song. The Lord rebuked them. "My children lie drowning in the sea. And you would sing?" Frequently this story is taken to mean that God loves Egyptians as well as Israelites and thus is sorrowful at the sight of their perishing. That is surely part of the truth. The deeper meaning may be that God cannot save Israelites without killing Egyptians.

Do you not see an echo of the story of the wheat and the weeds here? The farmer said, "Don't try to pull the weeds out; you will kill some of the wheat." In the very act of rooting out evil, something of value is also damaged. God's judgment in history seems caught up in this same dilemma. In order to liberate Israel from bondage, God destroys Egyptians. God loves Egyptians too.

An incident in the New Testament implies a similar truth. When King Herod heard that the Messiah had been born, he gave the order that all the male children two years old and under who lived in the vicinity of Bethlehem should be killed (Matthew 2:16). The very sending of the Savior into the world indirectly causes the death of innocent babies and brings about great weeping and lamenting among their mothers and fathers. Granted, it was Herod who gave the order to murder. The fact is that had not the Messiah been born, the children would not have died. The heart of a loving God surely was broken at the sight of drowning Egyptians in the Red Sea and of dying babies in Judea. The conclusion would seem to be that in order to be involved in our lives, to judge the wicked and save the helpless, God is implicated in violence. Thus is God also caught up in the complexities, ambiguities, and trade-offs that perplex and frustrate us.

Reinhold Niebuhr suggests that the perfect love of God can be symbolized only by Jesus becoming powerless on the cross. There he is physically and symbolically above the vicissitudes of actual life and history. The power of Jesus on the cross is found only in the persuasiveness of a life fully surrendered to God. Jesus in the marketplace is caught up in the same ambiguities that we are. Jesus was asked whether it was right to pay taxes to Caesar. He could only say that it was proper to render to Caesar what is Caesar's and to God what is God's (Matthew 22:15-22). This is an answer that is no answer to the particular issues involved. It was the only reply he could give without participating in the compromises and trade-offs that we face every day.

What shall we conclude from all this? Does the fact that wheat and weeds are so entangled that we cannot do good without also doing evil mean that we should do nothing? Shall we simply sit down while we wait for heaven? No, I think not. This parable does not contain the whole truth of Scripture nor the whole counsel of the gospel. Its message is not that we cannot make things better. It is only a warning that we cannot make them perfect.

This parable was originally intended to refute those Christians who wanted to have a pure Church, free from all spiritual stain. The church, they said, should be made up of saints only, the righteous and untainted. Throw the sinners out. The message of this parable on that score is loud and clear. Saints and sinners cannot so easily be distinguished from one another. Wheat and weeds grow in the lives of all.

His name was Otis Perkins. We all called him Mr. Doog. He was the community drunk. Doog was a good man who, everybody said, would give you the shirt right off his back if you needed it. Now and then he went on a big drinking spree. Sometimes he would end up drunk lying in the grass behind our barn. He would talk, endlessly and loudly. He spoke of many things. More than once I heard him recite how he was thrown out of New Hope Baptist Church for being a drunkard. Well, all that happened years and years ago, but he still remembered. The pain was still there, and it was deep. The good folks at New Hope were trying to maintain standards. That is a good thing to do. How can you do it without assuming that the wheat and the weeds can be neatly separated? How can you do it without leaving deep wounds in the likes of Mr. Doog Perkins, the community drunk? The church is in a dilemma. It would be a perversion of the Bible as a whole to conclude that all attempts to have standards of church membership should be abandoned.

So it is in other realms of life. The fact that we cannot free ourselves from all risk and failure does not suggest that there is nothing we can do to make our lives more tolerable and satisfying.

Even if all reforms in society are partial failures and even if perfect justice is always a hope and not an achievement, this does not imply that all efforts to make things better are futile. Because we cannot make absolute distinctions between good and evil does not imply that relative differences between right and wrong are impossible.

In the Church, in society, and in our individual lives, we have to live with partial successes and partial failures, with compromises and trade-offs. We gain something we want at the expense of something else that is good. Sometimes we have to be content with a little gain here and a little gain there and sometimes no gain at all and a setback now and then. You win some, and you lose some. That's life. The perennial problem is to live joyfully before God and one another without giving up or giving in. The challenge is to live lovingly before God and others without becoming complacent about the suffering around us or despairing because the battle against injustice and misery seems never to be won. The goal is to live faithfully before God and each other, accepting and enduring those stubborn afflictions in our own lives without cynicism or bitterness. The hope is that we can all live before God and each other in constant alertness to find those places where what cannot be made perfect for all can at least be made better for some with the least damage to the rest.

None of this is to deny that radical change may be called for at times. Revolution and not evolution may be God's order for the day with all the risks and possibilities that entails. The rule always is: the most that can be done for the sake of greater justice should be done. The faithful disciple of Jesus moves between complacency and despair in love and in hope to do for the neighbor the best that is possible under the circumstances. The obedient disciple seeks to be wise in discerning what that is.

Joy and sorrow, laughter and tears, success and failure, surprise and disappointment, triumph and tragedy, victory and defeat — these opposites are interwoven like wheat and weeds in the soil of our lives. They grow together in perplexing and unpredictable ways. In this adventure we have each other for mutual support. We live in companionship with God who suffers and triumphs with us in a kingdom that is always coming in wonder and surprise to bring new life and joy in ways beyond our knowing.

---

1. Lawrence Ferlinghetti, *A Coney Island Of The Mind* (New York: New Directions, 1958), p. 89.

The Reign Of Christ In A Complicated World

Ephesians 1:15-22; Acts 1:6-11

Drugs, children killing children in schools, AIDS, terrorism, torture of dissidents, abortion, earthquakes, hurricanes, pollution, capital punishment, nuclear waste, acid rain, crime, refugees, population explosion, global warming, destruction of the ozone, rape, cancer, Alzheimer's disease, violence against homosexuals, cholesterol, threat of nuclear war, homelessness, taxes, poverty, starving children in Africa, teenage pregnancy, suicide, euthanasia, divorce, child abuse, and on and on. Problems, problems, problems — and what has the reign of Christ to do with all that?

The text in Acts speaks of the ascension of Jesus. He promises that the disciples will be clothed with power from on high. This power will enable them to go to the ends of the earth proclaiming the gospel and doing good works. The first chapter of Ephesians declares that all things have been put under the feet of the exalted Christ, whose name is above every name. This is an exhilarating passage. It speaks of the reign of Christ through the Spirit making hope alive. The Spirit enlightens the eyes of the heart that believers may know the immeasurable greatness of God's power. They will discern the working of divine might when Christ was raised from the dead to sit at the right hand of God in heavenly places. The beauty of this text makes the pulse race. But I repeat, what has the reign of Christ to do with the problems that beset the world? If all things have been put under the feet of Christ, why have the kingdoms of this world not yet become the kingdom of our Lord?

Surrounded by so many problems, we are likely to be filled with a sense of bafflement that is well nigh overwhelming. Our perplexity is well grounded and for at least three reasons.

First, there are so many problems. The list is endless. To all the social difficulties we already had, we have recently added another set. We have learned to speak of ecology and of environmental issues. This new awareness began to grow a little more than three decades ago. My daughter Melissa helped imprint this on my consciousness. She was about four years old at the time. We were riding into Philadelphia across the Penrose Avenue bridge between the airport and center city. On either side of us were huge refineries belching their flames and smoke. From this high point we could get a glimpse of modern industrial society in miniature. The smell of the refineries penetrated the closed windows. Melissa got a whiff. She said one word, "Pollution." I realized at once that a new era had begun. Had I viewed this sight when I was a child, I would have been impressed with the industrial productivity these refineries and factories represented. I would have taken satisfaction in the wealth all this activity produced. Not Melissa. Her brief analysis epitomized the new consciousness of a younger generation.

Previously, we had thought it tough enough to achieve prosperity, economic progress, and efficiency under conditions of justice. Now to all that we have to worry whether unrestrained growth will kill us. We wonder whether a prosperous society is compatible with a sustainable one. At the world level the question can be put like this: How can we achieve an ecologically and economically sustainable world order that is just? Can we produce enough food and other necessities for an expanding population? And can we do so without polluting ourselves to death or exhausting essential resources? Closer to home we have become acutely conscious of waste and pollution. We are realizing how much our high consumption rates contribute to the depletion of the world's resources. We are recognizing how all this adds to the growing pile of garbage and hazardous waste materials.

It has been more than thirty years since Melissa got a whiff of Philadelphia and pronounced her one-word verdict — pollution.

Who can doubt that the threat posed by a contaminated environment will increasingly be at the top of the nations's agenda during the twenty-first century?

In the second place, the problems we face are complex. Our difficulties have no simple answers. We live in a complicated world. Take the problem of world hunger. Investigation would show that producing and distributing enough food involves patterns of world trade, population growth in the poor countries, special problems of agriculture in tropical regions, climate, geography, economic incentives for farmers, cultural attitudes toward having children, political rivalries, civil wars, transportation facilities inside needy areas, and a host of other baffling obstacles.

If you ask the experts, they disagree. Their answers reflect not only their technical knowledge but also their political commitments and cultural values. Liberals blame the affluent countries for the plight of the poor ones. Conservatives locate the fault in the attitudes, values, and social arrangements of the poverty stricken peoples themselves. How is the average Christian to know who is right about all this? We can give money to help those overseas and contribute to food banks at home. Beyond that, how can we be sure what national and global changes are either necessary or possible? Most of us have enough trouble keeping our checkbooks balanced.

My office was on the third floor before I retired. One day I brought a sandwich and some fruit for lunch. To keep it cool, I put my baloney and my apple on a ledge outside my window. During the morning a strong gust of wind apparently came along and blew it off. At lunch time I retrieved a badly battered sandwich and a splattered apple from the shrubbery three floors down. As I held the mangled remains in my hands, I thought to myself, "If I cannot preserve my lunch for a few hours, how can I resolve the population explosion and save the world from environmental disaster?"

In the third place, a deeply frustrating feature of social problem-solving is the inevitable fact of trade-offs. We have all learned that there is no free lunch. The mouse who thinks otherwise is in for a surprise when taking the cheese from the trap. Everything has a cost. With every rose are many thorns. Every proposed solution achieves gains at the expense of undesirable effects. No response achieves all good results and eliminates all the bad. We have to optimize the good and minimize the bad to get a tolerable compromise in which everybody wins a little bit. Illegal drugs are a scourge on our society today. Far more people die from the use of tobacco and alcohol than from cocaine. Nevertheless, the destruction of lives caused by the outlawed varieties of drugs is immense. But what shall we do? Get tough, say most. Provide more resources for catching the violators. Make the penalties more severe. Yet the more money we spend on law enforcement, the greater the drug traffic seems to get. Legalize drugs and spend more on prevention and rehabilitation, say a minority. Huge sums now devoted to law enforcement could be devoted to other needs. We could work harder at keeping people off drugs. Crime and violence would certainly be reduced. However, the number of addicts might increase for an indefinite time. Legalizing drugs might attract drug users from other countries. No solution exists that does not have a catch.

Every proposal to reduce defense spending and close obsolete military bases raises a cry that people will be put out of jobs. Giving preference to women and minorities creates job opportunities for groups that have long been treated unjustly. At the same time it may penalize white males. As individuals, they also deserve a chance. They may have little personal responsibility for the wrongs of the past. Legislators have recently been debating whether teenage girls should be required to have parental permission, or at least notify them, before they can have an abortion. It seems that parents ought to know about such a serious thing. Schools require parental consent for matters much less important. But getting parents involved would trap some young girls in desperate circumstances. It might force them to bear an unwanted child with terrible consequences. Parent-daughter relationships already strained might be further damaged. Yet some girls who were forced to tell their parents unexpectedly found them supportive. The result was a strengthening of daughter-parent ties. Having the law will do damage in some cases and not having the law will have bad consequences in other situations.

We could indefinitely extend this list of problems that offer no perfect resolution but only painful trade-offs. Jesus captured this truth in a story about the wheat and the weeds growing together. Their roots are so intertwined that any effort to pull out the weeds destroys some of the wheat (Matthew 13:24-30). That's the way it is in this life. No wonder these questions are controversial. But have you noticed that most people hold up only one side of these complicated issues? Most of the time the issues get presented as right versus wrong, truth versus error. That is too simplistic. Often, one right confronts another right. Frequently, it is a matter of one partial truth against another partial truth. But to recognize how complicated things are makes decision-making difficult. So we are confused and find ourselves baffled.

Returning to our theme, we conclude that it is necessary to speak of the embattled reign of Christ. The exalted Christ confronts powers that postpone the day when all enemies will be put down. Stubborn facts, social inertia, and recalcitrant institutions obstruct the coming of the Commonwealth of God on earth. Moreover, the complexity that requires compromise makes progress ambiguous. So we work and struggle for limited gains in justice. We strive for some relative improvement in the human lot. We live in hope, neither giving up nor giving in. We live in confidence that what cannot be made perfect can be made better for some people. We rejoice in every evidence of progress toward health and prosperity despite the persistence of oppression and misery.

And what shall be our stance as we seek to ally ourselves with the embattled reign of Christ on earth? Three brief suggestions may point the way toward a responsible life.

First our all, we live in the context of grace. We are justified from our sins. We are also justified from our bafflement and perplexity in the midst of stubborn trade-offs. Grace covers us when we can do good only by creating additional evil. The necessity of political compromise means that purity of action is impossible. The grace-filled Christian does not go into the world out of guilt. Believers do not labor under the burden of having to save the world by relentless effort. Guilt paralyzes. Bearing the burdens of the whole world all the time leads to despair. The assurance of living by grace sets us free to be ourselves, accepted and affirmed as we are with all our limits. But it sets us free to be responsible, to use our energy to do what we can in loving service to our neighbors in the pursuit of justice. We go out to battle the demonic powers neither blinded by tears of guilt nor crushed to earth by obligation to save the world or else be doomed and damned. Rather we go in the joyous freedom of the daughters and sons of God. Out of gratitude for the gift of life and its goodness, we seek to increase the enjoyment and ecstasy of us all.

In the second place, we have to make responsibility manageable. We cannot seek solutions to all problems or take part in every good cause. The days do not have enough hours for that. Recently, for a number of reasons, my financial situation improved somewhat. I decided to increase my giving to a number of agencies I thought were doing good work. Also, I added a few that I had not supported previously. You can guess what happened. In the next few weeks, I was deluged by letters from all sorts of groups and causes wanting me to contribute. It was obvious that my name was being freely passed around. They must swap mailing lists. The point is that I could not give to all these groups even if I knew all of them to be worthy. There is no end to good causes.

We can select a few and support them. Groups can form in churches that focus on some particular area that needs attention — hunger, prisons, homelessness, and so on. A rule of thumb might be that every church member will be involved in working in and supporting at least one good cause from which that person does not directly benefit. We can make responsibility manageable by selecting some part of the total universe of possible good works. We can give time, energy, and money to a few of them. We can help make the reign of Christ more real in some portion of the world.

Finally, we can seek to discern the signs of the times to locate where the growing edges of progress are. We can commit our efforts where they will count. Now and then right and ripe moments appear in which a moral breakthrough can occur. A fortunate group of historical forces converge to make possible what could not have happened before. History becomes pregnant with new possibilities of justice and liberation. Two centuries ago on this continent a new nation was born. It asserted the equality of all people. It announced that all human beings have certain rights that no government can take away. A century later, history was pregnant with forces that led to the abolition of slavery. A breakthrough occurred a generation ago in the civil rights movement led by Martin Luther King, Jr. In 1990 and afterward new birth was taking place in Eastern Europe. The breakup of the Soviet Union raises new hopes and introduces new perils.

Always we need to be asking ourselves two questions. 1) What is history pregnant with in the town, state, and nation where I live? 2) How can I become a midwife of the Commonwealth of God assisting in the birth of the new and the better? The answer to these questions provides a clue to how our own efforts may increase the reign of Christ in a complicated world.

One Of These Days[1]

Psalm 103; Matthew 6:25-32

It was not what he said. It was that he said it at the right moment that made a remark of Marvin Brown stand out in my memory for more than 45 years. What he said was obvious. Saying it when he did made an indelible impression on me. The scene was a Baptist church in a small Georgia town. As the presiding minister I was leading a funeral procession to the church cemetery. Marvin Brown was one of the pallbearers carrying the body of a long-time resident of that little town to his final resting place. We walked in silence. The only sounds were the noise of our feet upon the grass and the din of traffic on the Atlanta highway in the distance. As we walked along, the silence was broken by the voice of Marvin Brown. He said, "You know, every one of us will have to make this journey one of these days." The silence returned. We walked on toward the grave.

When my children were little, we were in Georgia. While we were there, we went to visit my wife's aunt who was in a nursing home. It was a sad and distressing sight to see her. She could hardly walk. She could hardly speak. Gone was the sparkle in her eyes. Gone was the crispness in her voice. It hardly seemed like the same person. All around her were other women in various states of disintegration. Two sat playing cards. Another sat silently at a table alone. Another cried out for a nurse to come wash her face. Still another babbled incoherently. The smell in the air was evidence that someone's diaper had just been changed. Some old woman who had once changed diapers on her own children was now herself reduced to the dependency of babyhood. Hands that had cared for others were feeble and trembling now. Bodies that had once been young and strong and healthy were withering away. The flowers were fading. It was like every nursing home you have ever been in. More recently three of my aunts, more than one cousin, and other relatives have lived their last days in a nursing home that became very familiar to me. Still later, with much reluctance, one sad day I took my mother and father to that same institution. My dad died five months later. As of this writing early in 2001, my mother is still there, gradually weakening.

The nursing home I refer to was just around the corner from the house where my parents lived for 37 years before they got too old to live alone any longer. One day a car stopped in their driveway. The driver came to the door and asked for directions to this very nursing home nearby. In the back seat was a thin, little, grey-haired old woman looking very frightened. We knew where she and that car were heading. My Aunt Rosalie said, after she was a resident there, "A nursing home is where you go to wait to die."

Again and again I have thought of Marvin Brown and of the journey that we must all take one of these days.

Yet it is not such observations as this that are the clearest reminders of our mortality. Our most intimate knowledge of the certainty of death comes in those moments now and then when without warning the fact that we are going to die hits us sharply in the gut. A wave of acute anxiety rips through us like a jagged knife. We are shaken with the startling clarity that Marvin Brown's observation applies to us. One day we will cease to be.

The fact of death needs not be established with proof for it is our most certain knowledge. The Psalmist was right. We are like grass. For a time it flourishes. Then the wind blows over the place, and it is no more. What shall we do with the inevitable fact of our dying? Should our attention be focused on the question of what happens after we die? That is an important matter for another time. For this occasion I want to focus on the implication of the fact of our dying some day for the here and now. What does it mean for our daily living that one of these days we will take that journey?

I wish to make two very simple points. A certain obviousness hovers about both of them. Nevertheless, I dare say that if you, if I, took them seriously, our lives might be very different from now on. If every day each of us could manage to accomplish two simple goals, the quality of our lives would be greatly improved. Having made that bold claim, let me proceed.

In the first place, the fact that we will die sometime enhances the value of our common experience every day. The philosopher Alfred North Whitehead said that the greatest evil in life is that time is "perpetual perishing." What he meant is that life is made up of a series of moments which come to be and pass away. The farther we move away from an experience, the dimmer it gets. The zest and freshness and vividness fade away until only a shadow of the past remains. We cannot possess any joy or pleasure forever. Time is "perpetual perishing." No matter how vivid the experience, the reality of the moment cannot be held before the imagination for all time in all its fullness and intensity. Inevitably the passing days gradually erode the memory. It slips gradually into the dim recesses of the past. Never again will it live in the completeness and vividness of its immediate reality. Yes, the sad truth is that time is "perpetual perishing." We cannot possess the joy of any moment forever. It fades away.

As true as that is, I do not agree with the great philosopher that this is the greatest evil. There is a greater evil I believe. It is true that I cannot remember today with the same intensity and vividness how the pecan pie I ate last week tasted at the moment. That exquisite flavor I enjoyed then cannot be recaptured now. Each passing day there is a loss that cannot be recovered. What is sadder still, however, is that there will come a time in which there will be no pecan pie in my future. Whitehead was wrong. The greatest evil is not that memories of previous pleasures fade. The greater evil is that a time comes when they can no longer be repeated. I can live with the fading memory of how pecan pie tasted last week, if I can enjoy that marvelous delight again next week. One day for me, for all of us, there will be no more future, no more expectation that the joys we have known can be repeated anymore on this earth.

What does death mean anyway? It means that we cease to have a future. Every year the faculty of the seminary gathered for commencement. When we were taking off our robes after the occasion, someone was likely to say, "Well, one more, and one less!" And so it is with every joy, with every satisfaction, every positive experience we have. Every day we live means one more, and one less. So the passing of time brings a double evil. It fades the memory of yesterday's pleasures and reduces the number of tomorrows in which they may be repeated. Hence, I say that the fact of our dying one day enhances the value of every present moment. It makes every minute precious. It makes every opportunity count. It makes every new experience a joy to be savored to the fullest. Life is now. Life is today. Enjoy it to the fullest and in all its robust flavor. Take it in all its richness, its fullness, and completeness: the sight of a sunset, a game of Frisbee™, the sound of a waterfall, the touch of a lover's caress, the taste of honey, the comforting word of a friend, the laughter of a child at play, the melody of your favorite song, the beauty of the grandest music. All the variety of the everyday simple pleasures takes on a new intensity and value when we experience them in the knowledge that time is "perpetual perishing." Time finally sweeps all before it like the wind takes away the flower that blooms and fades and is no more.

There is a moving passage in Thornton Wilder's play *Our Town* that makes the point in a vivid way. Emily, who had died, is given a chance to go back and live one day of her life over again. She chooses her twelfth birthday. What impresses Emily most as she appears in her mother's kitchen is how much there is to life. She suddenly realizes how sweet and precious are all the simple things, the ordinary sights and sounds and smells of everyday life — a ticking clock, coffee, hot baths, newly-ironed dresses, sleeping and waking up. It all goes so fast, and we miss so much of it without ever knowing it. She concludes, "And oh, earth, you're too wonderful for anybody to realize you. Do any human beings ever realize life while they live it?" The Stage Manager replies, "No, the saints and poets, maybe — they do some."[2]

Well, we cannot all be saints and poets. We can try to live every day in the awareness that one day we must take that journey of which Marvin Brown spoke. If we can, maybe everyday life will take on more meaning. The ordinary things will be more precious. We will realize more of life than we ordinarily do.

I have not lived in Georgia since I was 31 years of age. I have now passed my seventy-first birthday. It has always been my hope and plan to return to the state of my birth to live out my last years. One of many reasons is that I carry memories of small sights, sounds, and feelings from my childhood. I would like to experience them again day by day and not just on those brief visits back. I think immediately of the feel of a clear, cold January night with the stars shining brightly, the feel of a crisp morning in March when Spring is already pushing the winter away, the sight of azaleas in nearly every yard in April, the sweet aroma of honeysuckle, the smell of hickory smoke from a fireplace in December, the sound of the wind sweeping through a grove of pine trees, the mingled chorus of the songs of a thousand insects on an August night punctuated by the croaking of frogs, the taste of old-fashioned pork barbecue, and on and on.

If I ever live there again, I know that those simple delights of the senses will be ever more meaningful because of the awareness that time grows short for their enjoyment. If we are wise, we will all begin now to savor the little things that make us happy before we all have to take the journey of which Marvin Brown spoke.

The second point is as simple as the first. It is this. The knowledge that one day we will die magnifies the importance of making decisions now. Today is opportunity day. Today is decision time. Life is full of choices. Every day we come to points in the road where there is a divide. We can only go one way. We have to choose. And then there are those more important turning points, those tougher choices that stay with us a while. We are tempted to postpone, to put off until tomorrow. Meanwhile, life goes on. We drift. The opportunity is gone. Everyone's list will be different. All of us have before us now choices that affect our lives, decisions we need to make and make now. The time has come to stop smoking, to begin exercising, to start a diet, to quit a job, to do a better job of what we are now doing, to propose a marriage, to end a marriage, to improve a marriage, to write a letter home, to break a bad habit, to make reconciliation with an estranged friend, to get angry with a friend who is bugging you, to break out of depression and passivity and take charge of our lives in some responsible way, to do something for the sake of justice in the world, for the burdened to stop acting like they are Atlas with the world on their shoulders and to throw the burden off, for the careless and irresponsible to pick up some of the burden, and on and on the list could go.

Each of us will have to complete the list for herself or himself. The implication is clear: whatever turning point you face — decide now, decide today, do it.

Do not misunderstand me. I am not urging impulsive or irresponsible plunging forward without thought. President Gorbachev quoted an old Russian proverb: "Measure seven times; cut only once." A bundle of wisdom lies hidden in the aphorism that we should look before we leap. Yes, but what about those of us who have come to the ditch and looked and backed away? We have summoned our courage and come back and looked longer. Then we back away again. What about those of us who have looked and looked and looked and looked and looked but have never leaped? Of course, we should consider alternatives carefully and use our reason and experience and the counsel of others as best we can. Finally, there comes a time to quit looking and start leaping. At last, there comes a moment to make a choice and live with it. The alternative is to drift our lives away in indecision and passivity. Opportunity knocks once, and sometimes twice or even maybe three times. It does not knock forever. So decide. Decide today.

The Psalmist contrasts the transitoriness of human life with the everlasting love of God. Jesus in the Sermon on the Mount contrasts the anxious fretting about food, drink, and clothing with the possibility of living trustfully before God. The Psalmist points us to the love of God. Jesus points us to the Commonwealth of God. He urges us to believe that if we set our minds first on God's providential care, we can live a day at a time without worrying about tomorrow. With that kind of faith we can live each moment, each hour, each day to the fullest as we approach that final journey which we all must make.

Some years ago I was in Georgia visiting my parents. One afternoon we decided to ride over to the little church where I had been pastor. When we got there, I said, "Let's go by the cemetery. That's one way of catching up on some of the news." So we did. I walked from grave to grave. Here and there I saw the name of some person who had been an active member of the church 25 years ago. I paused a minute to remember each of them. Then one grave caught my eye in a special way. I read the words on the stone.

Marvin Brown
February 17, 1971

I remembered once again the words he had spoken not many yards from where I now stood looking at his grave. Marvin Brown had taken his journey.

While there is still time, let us begin to enjoy the ordinary pleasures of every day. While there is still time, let us make the decisions that life requires. We are all now many years closer to the journey that we all must take than we were when Marvin Brown was carried to his final resting place. So let us live to the fullest, beginning now — while there is still time.

---

1. An earlier version of this sermon was published in *Pulpit Digest* (May-June 1981), pp. 21-24. Reprinted with permission from *Pulpit Digest*, copyright Logos Productions Inc. (800-328-0200).

2. Thornton Wilder, *Our Town* (New York: Coward McCann, Inc., 1938), pp. 124-125.

Why Roman Soldiers Love The Sermon On The Mount

Matthew 5:38-48; Matthew 26:6-13

Every now and then someone suggests that it would be wonderful if everyone lived by the Sermon on the Mount. Well, it would be wonderful for thieves, bullies, lazy Roman soldiers, and people who borrow money with no intention of paying it back. Someone breaks into your house. Do not resist. Someone strikes you on the cheek. Turn the other one. A Roman soldier forces you to go one mile with his belongings. Go with him the second mile. Someone with quite shaky credit wants to borrow some money. Lend without asking questions.

If everybody lived by these ideals, there would not be people breaking into your house or empires based on forced conscription of civilian labor or dishonest borrowers. But in the world we live in, it would be wonderful for some people if everybody else lived by the Sermon on the Mount — wonderful for criminals, cheaters, and violent people. Live by the Sermon on the Mount? Are you kidding?

What are we to do with these hard sayings? Since they were given to us by Jesus, we agree that something important is being said. What do they mean? Are they to be taken literally? If so, consequences follow that are disastrous for ordered, civilized living. If we do not take them literally, are we betraying Jesus by watering them down so that they lose their clout? Christians have wrestled with these hard sayings for centuries. They stand out in their stark absoluteness with all their uncompromising demands.

They leave us to make of them what we can. It may help to examine some of the ways Christians have interpreted them in the past.

It is because they put impossible demands on us, say some, that they are valuable. The very purpose of these sayings is to show that before the law, we are condemned. They bring us to our knees as sinners who have no hope unless God accepts us as we are and forgives us. Law is the iron rod that drives us to the grace of Christ. Certainly the notion that we are saved not by our good works but by the free gift of God is a strong note in the New Testament. But does this viewpoint win too easy a victory? If the demands are simply impossible, that may lead to complacency. They lose any power to require anything of us and may lead to a reliance on "cheap grace" (Bonhoeffer).

A second approach is that these hard sayings assume that the world will end soon. The usual responsibilities do not hold. Ordinary duties can be foregone, since the world will not last very long anyway. Hence, we are free to show extraordinary love to whoever happens to confront us in the moment. Jesus apparently did believe that this age was running out very soon. Since we do not live in the expectation of the imminent end of things, we have to reinterpret these sayings for our own time. Maybe so, but how much should we make of the point?

Let us suppose that I am on my way to a nearby village with life-saving medicine for people who have been struck by an epidemic. A Roman soldier confronts me and forces me to carry his things a mile. Shall I volunteer to take them a second mile while people die waiting for the medicine I have for them? No, I think not. Only the certainty that the world will end before I could get to the village will suffice to suspend my obligation to save lives. The mere possibility that the world will end in the near future is not enough to eliminate ordinary, short-term responsibilities.

A third and more promising alternative arises. These sayings assume that we have only one neighbor to be responsible for. Therefore, we can serve that person without reservation. Once other people come into the picture, the whole situation is changed. We have to decide how to distribute our love among many neighbors. Let us go back to the example. I may properly refuse to go the second mile with the Roman soldier in order to get the medicine to the sick people in the next town. I have many neighbors to be concerned about. I cannot give my full attention and loving service to the soldier who happens to be right here right now.

Maybe we are on the right track now. Nevertheless, before we assume the problem is solved, let us take one more look. Assume that we eliminate any responsibilities that I have for other people. I am alone with only myself to take care of. Am I under obligation to go the second mile? To turn the other cheek? To lend money to anybody? According to many Protestant theologians of the last generation, we can make a good case for saying yes to these questions. Christian love, they say, is heedless of the self. It sacrifices the self for the sake of the neighbor. It gives all to the other without any thought for being loved in return. The commandment that we should love our neighbor as we love ourselves really means, love your neighbor *instead* of yourself. You know how you love yourself? Well, that is the way you should love your neighbor.

This self-denying, sacrificial love is the kind that Jesus had. It is love that led him to the cross. It is the self-giving love we are obligated to demonstrate to our neighbors. Sacrificial love is unconcerned about what it costs us. It does not consider what we might get in return. Greater love has no one than the person who lays one's life down for a friend (John 15:13). We are to love with no regard for the merit of another. God shows love for us in that while we were yet sinners, Christ died for us (Romans 5:8). Everywhere in the New Testament love is utterly self-giving. It sacrifices the self for the sake of the other. That seems to be the idea of love that is present in the Sermon on the Mount.

Before we conclude the matter, let us go a step further. Consider the examples again and heighten them. Suppose the Roman soldier makes me go not one mile but ten miles and finally forces me to become his permanent slave. Do I willingly serve him without protest? Suppose I turn the other cheek and the bully not only strikes it but also knocks me down and beats me with a stick. Do I put up no resistance? Suppose I have lent out all the money I have. Do I go to the bank and borrow so that I can make more loans to people who may never pay me back? Suppose the would-be borrower is rich and I am poor? Do I lend that person money too? An intruder breaks in and threatens to kill me. Am I to be totally nonresisting even if the opportunity arises to save my life by hitting him over the head?

Is there no point at which I draw the line? Are the poor to sacrifice for the rich? Are the sick to sacrifice for the healthy? Are the powerless to serve the powerful without restriction? Am I utterly forbidden to take myself, my needs and wants, into account? Am I always to sacrifice without any limit for the sake of the other, no matter what?

To say yes to all these questions leads to unacceptable and even contradictory conclusions. The very purpose of love is to benefit people, to serve needs, to reduce suffering, to liberate, to set the oppressed free. But if in serving my neighbor, I end up oppressed, humiliated, and degraded, love's very mission is destroyed. I too am a person. If my needs are denied, if I am destroyed, then the community of equals united by bonds of love in the praise of God is undermined. I am to love my neighbor because my neighbor is a person of great value. I too am a person of great worth, for whom Christ also died. Surely God counts the need and value of one person equal to that of any other person. Surely my just interests are worth defending, even if I have to defend them myself. To take these hard sayings literally would lead to the denial of the very community of free and equal persons that love itself seeks. To understand love in terms of self-sacrifice is offensive to justice, which love itself craves.

Let us see, then, if we can make a fresh start. At the outset I want to say right out loud that I know of no interpretation of the Sermon on the Mount that is without difficulties. Every attempt to relate these hard sayings to the complexities of human life in this world runs into trouble at some point. All I can say is that this is the best I have been able to figure out up to now. One place to begin is with the commandment that we love our neighbor as we love ourselves. Three points can be quickly made.

The first is that we are to regard our neighbor's need equal to our own, no less and no more. That is a very high demand in and of itself. The Christian motivated by such love seeks a community of free and equal persons mutually devoted to the good of each and of all. Individuals are united by love in the common pursuit of goods to be justly shared. The ideal is that people should show equal regard for each other.

The second point is that my regard for my neighbor is to be absolute, unconditional, and unrelenting. No matter what the other person does, I must continue to honor the worth of that person and promote that person's fair interest in the life of the community. My obligation to meet the needs of the other person and to promote the welfare of all my neighbors continues under all circumstances, no matter what everybody else is doing.

My obligation to consider the neighbor's good equal to my own never ceases. If someone breaks into my house, this does not mean I should be totally unresisting. It means that in defending my just interests, I am not to forget that the intruder is a person made in the image of God for whom Christ died. I am not to hate that person. I am not to seek revenge, not to resist beyond what is actually necessary to protect my own worth and value as a child of God for whom Christ also died. My neighbor's good remains equal to my own. I am to seek that good even if the neighbor is an intruder with violent intentions. But my own needs and my own good do not cease to matter either. Hence, I am not required to let others utterly destroy me or oppress me or subject me to their own unjust demands or exploit me without limit. Yet in resisting, I continue to regard the would-be oppressor as a person whose own real needs and basic welfare matter equally with my own.

Finally, in the third place, Christian love is not sacrificial by nature. It becomes sacrificial when my neighbor's need exceeds my own or when the greater good of the community takes precedence over my own particular interest. The Christian takes the initiative to promote the other person's good, no matter what everyone else is doing. But he or she resists when the other person tries to deny his or her own equally valid interest in the goods of this life. Love is sacrificial when the situation calls for it. It is protective of the just interests of everybody, including one's own self, when attacked. Always and without ceasing, Christian love seeks justice for all in a community of free and equal persons.

Whether this helps to get some perspective on the hard sayings of the Sermon on the Mount, you must judge. It is the best I can come up with for now. I have been led to one other conclusion. Love has many facets. It lives in multidimensional splendor. In particular, it assumes two forms relevant for the issue at hand. I call them the *ecstatic* and the *ethical* dimensions of love. In making my three points just now, I was speaking of Christian love in its *ethical* form. Here we have to measure, count, and distribute in accordance with rules in order to treat everyone justly. We have to decide between competing claims to make sure that all get what they are due without anyone being left out or treated unfairly. In ethics we make choices that involve trade-offs and compromises. We calculate and make intuitive judgments about where one's just interest ends and another takes up. Love bids us to make the best ethical judgments we can in the light of the Christian ideal of a free and equal community of people united by love. This is the realm we live in most of the time when are trying to be Christians. This is the everyday world of stubborn facts and complex decision-making.

But love has another dimension. It sometimes rises to heights of joyful overflowing with affection and concern for another that goes beyond ethics. Love in the *ecstatic* mode bubbles and boils over with feelings of delight, passion, and pleasure in the very existence of the loved one. It is enthralled, thrilled, and captivated in the presence of the other. When we are in this mood, we want those we love to have the very best we can give them. We reach out to do everything we possibly can without hesitation, without counting the costs or looking for anything in return. We give ourselves in joyful abandon, lost in wonder, totally devoted to the needs and pleasures of those we love. We become excessive in the outpouring of affection, care, and undivided attention. We give all. We hold nothing back.

It is the love that parents sometimes feel for their children, that lovers have for each other in the height of passion. It is the love that we have for our friends in those precious moments of intimacy we share with those close to us. It is the kind of love the woman showed who poured the perfume on Jesus' feet. She was in an *ecstatic* mood, whereas the *ethically* minded disciples thought she should have sold the ointment to get money and buy food for the poor (Matthew 26:6-13). If we give beyond what reason would suggest and what justice would demand, it is not felt as a sacrifice. It is what we most want to do, what makes us happy, what fills us with overflowing joy. We give without restraint or without in the least worrying at the moment whether our devotion will be reciprocated. Love rarely reaches this *ecstatic* zenith of affectionate feelings. Most of the time we have to live in the *ethical* dimension in which we distribute our concern with care in order to have enough to go around and not leave anyone out or with less than they deserve.

Many passages about love in the New Testament persuade me that they were written in an *ecstatic* mood. Joyful abandon for the other is the most natural and spontaneous thing in the world when love overflows. It may help us to read the Sermon on the Mount if we think about what love would intend, feel, and do when caught up in the ecstatic regard for the other in which affection and desire to serve know no bounds in moments that scandalize justice and offend the careful cautions and calculations of cool reasonableness.

We cannot rise to the acme of spontaneous joy and overflowing regard for another by simply taking thought. But if we have by grace and good luck had the fortune of feeling the ecstasy of love in our own hearts for someone we care for unconditionally and without restraint, perhaps then we will know at least for a moment what Jesus was talking about in the Sermon on the Mount.

Peacemakers
As Troublemakers

Jesus — That Troublemaker!

Matthew 10:34-42; Luke 10:49-53

His loyalty to Jesus got him into one predicament after another. Don West rode up and down the highways of Georgia on his Indian Chief motorcycle more than a half century ago associating himself with revolutionary causes. He was born in the mountains of north Georgia among the poor people he loved and served for a lifetime. He was one of a small group of radical Christians in the South who yearned for a new order that would unite the races and deliver the destitute from oppression. West had the sensitive soul of a poet and the zeal of an Old Testament prophet. He learned the social gospel in the divinity school of Vanderbilt University, eventually earned a doctorate, and taught at Oglethorpe University.

Yet this poet, prophet, and preacher was chased from one town to another and tormented by factory owners, politicians, and newspaper editors. He was seen as a dangerous threat to the existing economic order — and he was. Yet all he wanted was justice for the poor. West found his inspiration in the teachings of Jesus. "Somehow," he said, "I can't help but preach the only Jesus I know, and he is a very bothersome fellow, and he gets me in Dutch time after time. Sometimes my wife may wish that I'd meet that other Jesus, the one most of the churches have up in the stained glass. But I just missed him somehow, and got tangled up with the one that stirred up the people. He's a powerful interesting guy, but bad medicine for a pastor in modern churches, or ancient ones either I reckon."[1] Don West tried to follow Jesus, and it got him into trouble.

Jesus seems to have anticipated that his followers might get into difficulty if they took him seriously. The text for today points in that direction. Jesus says, "Do not think I have come to bring peace on earth; I have not come to bring peace, but a sword" (Matthew 10:34). He goes on to say that he has come to set family members against one another. Loyalty to him must come before allegiance to mother and father or son and daughter. Those who are not willing to put him first even at the expense of alienation from family are not worthy of him. In the parallel text in Luke, Jesus says that he has come to cast fire on earth and to bring division among people (Luke 12:49-51). These are hard sayings indeed. They contradict what we would most naturally expect. Did not Jesus come to bring reconciliation, to unite people, to spread love and peace? Here he appears to say the very opposite. He brings not peace but a sword, not unity but division, not reconciliation but fire. What can these words possibly mean?

It is hard to believe that Jesus is expressing his direct and deliberate intention. Hence, I will play the role that preachers often assume and speak as if I know the mind of Jesus! My suggestion is that we can only make sense of these words and reconcile them to his total message and ministry if we assume that Jesus is speaking paradoxically. He appears to be offering a contradiction, yet his words contain deep truth. Jesus is not saying that his fundamental aim is to bring fire, division, and a sword. Rather he is acknowledging that his mission will inevitably set people against one another. Telling the truth, promoting goodness, loving to the fullest will lead to an outcome we wish to avoid but cannot. The opposite of what we hope for will happen. Jesus is aware that a positive mission can have negative side effects. And he dreads to see that come to pass.

He indicates this by his own words. "I came to cast fire on the earth; and would that it were already kindled! I have a baptism to be baptized with; and how I am constrained until it is accomplished!" (Luke 12:49-50). He is saying that some terrible things are going to happen. He wants to get it over with. What he does not intend will follow from what he does intend. This will be a painful experience that he dreads. How can it be that Jesus will produce the opposite of what he sets out to achieve? How can this be?

We can first simply observe that people were divided against each other in response to the ministry of Jesus. Some people thought he was the Messiah and followed him. Others not only refused to accept him as the Messiah but set about to kill him — and succeeded. We can readily understand how some might reject him or doubt him or just have nothing to do with him at all. But why would they kill him? Why would people kill a person who taught love, who preached good news to the poor, who went about doing good, who healed the sick, and who in every way sought to make life better?

Several centuries before Jesus was born, Plato, the Greek philosopher, offered an allegory that throws light on the subject at hand. Imagine, Plato said, a large cave. Inside, people are chained so that they can only see the rear wall. They cannot turn around to face the entrance. They have been there all their lives. The sun shines through the entrance to the cave and casts shadows of anything that passes by. The shadows dance on the back wall of the cave. During their lifetimes the prisoners get very good at making out the shadowy figures cast on the wall. They find a certain order and regularity in the movements and come to believe that what they see is the whole of reality.

Suppose one of the captives gets loose and turns around. At first he will be blinded by the light. He may even be afraid of what he sees. Suppose he manages to make his way toward the entrance to the cave. He will see that what he believed to be real is only a shadowy illusion. The genuine things in the world are those moving figures themselves. He had only seen their shadows on the wall. Moreover, he will see that the source of all light is the sun itself. It is the reason anything can be seen at all. The sun is so bright that it takes a long time for his eyes to adjust. All his life he had lived in near darkness and illusion. Yet he thought he knew what was true and real. Having been liberated from this shadowy world of appearances, he will appreciate the truth and the light. He will take special pleasure in the sun that is their source. In the New Testament the experience of turning from illusion to reality is defined as being "born again" or of being born from above (John 3).

Having seen the light, the liberated and transformed prisoner will want to go back into the cave and tell the remaining captives what he has found. Upon returning, he finds that he is not very good at judging the shadows on the wall anymore. His eyes, having become accustomed to the light, cannot see in the dark. The people in the cave are much better at making out what they see on the wall than this enlightened convert. When he tries to tell his companions what he has found outside, they do not believe him. Why he cannot even make out the shadows on the wall! How could he possibly have knowledge of a realm of light and truth beyond? Having been born again, he is no longer at home in the darkness of the cave. So the prisoners reject him as a madman who has no sense at all. They get so angry that some want to kill him.

Plato's allegory of the cave gives us insight into the sword and fire and division that Jesus brings to earth. Jesus comes with a message of light, of love, of truth. He tells of a coming kingdom in which the poor and the outcasts will be liberated. His message is from above, but many prefer the shadows on the wall that they have always lived by. They think the shadows are the reality. So Jesus is denounced. Some want to kill him. They do not believe that he brings a message from beyond the darkness they live in. They plot to get rid of him.

In April of 1968 another good man was killed. A sniper's bullet ended the life of Martin Luther King, Jr., on a motel balcony in Memphis, Tennessee. A previous attempt had been made on his life. He had already survived a stabbing with a knife. On the flight to Memphis, the pilot came on the intercom system to say that Dr. Martin Luther King, Jr., was on the plane. Special safety precautions had to be taken. He hoped the other passengers would be understanding and patient with the necessary delay this would cause. This Baptist preacher was the one who had stood up in Washington to speak of his dream. What was that dream? It was that all people would one day live in peace and harmony. Everywhere he spoke of justice and love. Everywhere he urged those who sought redress of grievances to do so non-violently. And everywhere somebody wanted to kill him. When someone finally succeeded, there were many who said that it was a shame that somebody had shot him.

But he was, after all, a troublemaker. For having a dream of justice for all and for preaching non-violent resistance to oppression and for upsetting the shadowy truths by which a segregated society had lived, he was hated and despised. His ministry brought a sword, caused division, and set fire upon the earth.

Clarence Jordan of Americus, Georgia, was another who brought fire and sword by advocating justice and living by love. He established a small community of non-violent people who lived in full equality, ignoring the accidents of class, race, nationality, and creed. I along with others from Mercer University visited Koinonia Farm one day. Clarence showed us the holes made by bullets fired right over the place where some in the community slept. Like Jesus and King, Clarence Jordan had seen a great light. Those who continued to live by the shadows on the wall thought he was crazy. Those who lived by the worldly wisdom of the age were quite good at making out the patterns they saw on the back of the cave. They simply could not understand what Clarence was talking about. He was an accomplished student of the Greek New Testament. He offered to study the Bible with his opponents. They could only see him as a dangerous influence, a threat to decency and order. The bright light of truth not only makes people who live in darkness turn away; it also makes them angry. It makes them violent. The shadowy deceptions by which an unjust society lives cannot stand the truth that exposes their illusions.

Jesus did not come with the deliberate intention of causing the sword to be drawn, of provoking families to split, of bringing fire upon earth. Yet the inevitable outcome of his mission to bring light, love, and truth was just that. Hence, we see irony in his words: "I will preach peace, but I will stir up conflict; I will teach love, and people will hate me for it!"

People still divide against one another when they confront Jesus. Madalyn Murray O'Hair was an atheist. Some years ago she brought a suit against prayer in the public schools. She said it was unconstitutional for her son to be forced to be present when prayer was offered. She won the case. Her son was then a teenager in school. He was the person in whose behalf Madalyn O'Hair brought the case. The son grew up and became a Christian. She remained an atheist. Mother was set against son. Their relationship was strained.[2]

People over the centuries have fought each other over who is the true representative of Jesus on earth today. Protestants and Catholics have persecuted each other in the past, each group believing it alone possessed the way, the truth, and the life. In Northern Ireland Protestants and Catholics still kill each other. In our own country Christians divide over abortion, over civil rights, over prayer in schools, over national defense, and over practically every other issue that has a moral dimension. Fundamentalists and liberals accuse each other of betraying Jesus.

During the turmoil over racial issues in the 1950s and 1960s churches were split into warring factions. Some pastors were forced out of pastorates for suggesting that segregation might be contrary to the will of God. Some time after the Supreme Court decision of 1954 outlawing segregation in the public schools, a group of socially liberal church people from all over the South met in Nashville. Their purpose was to coordinate their efforts to move toward racial equality. They had such a good time together that they decided to celebrate their unity and commitment to justice with a communion service. Well, that's when the fight began. As I recall, they finally were able to overcome their disarray by using a Canadian order of service. Here was a group of good Christians united in fighting injustice who exposed their own conflicts over who is authorized properly to break the bread at the Lord's Table. It is a strange world we live in.

Jesus was right when he said he came to bring division, a sword, and fire. He wants to see peace on earth. He knows that peacemakers are often the cause of wars. He wants to see love embodied in human relationships. He knows that those who love most fully stir up hatred among those who cannot face their own hypocrisies. Jesus wants to see people believe the truth. He knows that truth-bearers often bring pain to eyes so accustomed to darkness that they cannot tell right from wrong. Jesus sought to bring love, peace, and unity. The result was hate, conflict, and division. No wonder he wished it did not have to be that way. No wonder he wanted to have his baptism over with.

What can all this teach us today? It leaves us with a paradoxical truth about life. We cannot always have goodness and truth without painful side effects. Love can generate hate, and hate can generate hate. Peacemakers can stir up trouble, and troublemakers can cause turmoil. Bearers of truth can start a fire, and liars can kindle flames. That is the way it is.

Beyond that we need to look at another passage in the larger text. Jesus speaks of discerning the signs of the times. As believers, we have the task of interpreting what is going on in the world and deciding what it all means. So let us be as wise as we can be in discerning the signs of the times. If we are to be numbered among those who bring fire, sword, and division, let us make sure it will be because we are disciples of Jesus and not among his enemies.

---

1. Quoted in Anthony P. Dunbar, *Against The Grain: Southern Radicals And Prophets, 1929-1959* (Charlottesville: University Press of Virginia, 1981), pp. 211-212.

2. This account is based on an interview with Madalyn O'Hair and her son I heard in 1980. I do not know what happened between them since or what the present situation is. Later, she disappeared, and suspicion arose that harm may have come to her.

Two Ways To Get Crucified

Matthew 27:33-44

A generation ago liberals learned that while segregationists might be wrong, they are not dumb. In 1954 the Supreme Court declared segregation in the public schools unconstitutional. A few states tried to find a way around this ruling. Some individuals said they would not conform to this new interpretation of things. Liberals in the South urged everyone to obey the law. A little bit later Martin Luther King, Jr., began to engage in civil disobedience. It was proper, he said, to disobey an unjust law in obedience to a higher authority. The liberals who had previously urged obedience to the law as determined by the Supreme Court found themselves in a dilemma. Some did an about-face. They began to follow King in saying that only those laws that are just have to be obeyed. Segregationists pounced on this apparent inconsistency and began to ask in taunting fashion, "Are we supposed to obey the law or not? Make up your minds." And if Martin Luther King can decide on the basis of his conscience whether to obey laws he doesn't like, why can't segregationists appeal to that principle too?

Seeing the television version of *The Final Days* reminded me how complicated this gets. Some of those involved in the Watergate scandal suggested a parallel between their breaking the law and the civil rights demonstrators and anti-war activists who engaged in acts of civil disobedience. President Richard Nixon himself hinted that the atmosphere in which the Watergate incidents occurred was in part created by the protest movements of the '60s. He noted that civil disobedience had frequently been blessed from American pulpits.

We could argue for a long time about whether the Watergate burglars and the draft card burners are alike or different in trying to justify their acts. And we could get into long discussions about whether the segregationists and the civil rights demonstrators were on equal moral grounds when they resorted to civil disobedience. Here I would only propose that the law can be *broken from above*, and it can be *broken from below*. Laws can be violated by acts morally inferior to the standards required by law. They can also be disobeyed in obedience to imperatives that are ethically superior to the legal code. Very low morality and very high morality can get you in jail. It is very important to know the difference between breaking the law from below and breaking it from above.

Perhaps we can get a better perspective on these differences if we look for a moment at an event far removed from our own time. Outside the gates of Jerusalem stood three crosses. On either side was a common criminal. In the center was Jesus of Nazareth. From this cross we can learn a great deal. Paul vowed to know nothing and to preach nothing except Jesus Christ and him crucified. He urged that God has chosen to save those who believe through the folly of the cross.

I want to call attention to another dimension of truth that is symbolized by all three crosses together. When we ponder this scene, we become aware that there are two ways to incur the wrath of society. One way is to be very bad. The two thieves are witness to this. They had endangered the order and security of society by resorting to brute force, to threats of death and violence. When they were apprehended and brought to trial, all decent people agreed that they must pay for their crimes. Religious leaders and officers of the state approved of the sentence. No one doubted that justice was done when these two were put upon the cross. If everyone lived as these two men did, chaos would result. The honorable institutions of society and decent ways of making a living would be undermined. The preservation of the social order required that these very bad men be condemned.

The situation is different when we turn to the other cross, the one in the middle. There were some, indeed, who thought that Jesus was also a very bad man. Was he not a blasphemer who pretended to have the authority to forgive sins? Had he not claimed to be the Messiah? Some accused him of being a revolutionary who sought to overthrow the Roman government and make himself a ruler over his own kingdom. Certainly he was an agitator who stirred up the people and caused trouble. Nobody ought really to be crucified, but, after all, he was a disturber of the peace. So the argument might go. When the situation is analyzed closely, we see that Jesus was not put to death because he was very bad. He was crucified because he was very good.

Yet while he hung there on the cross, people passing by wagged their heads, derided him, and made fun of him. And you know what? The thieves reviled Jesus as well. What irony! The criminals said awful things to Jesus. How is it that the very worst people can make fun of the very best people and try to make them look bad? How mixed up things get in this crazy world of ours. Truth is indeed sometimes stranger than fiction.

Let us proceed with the story. We should notice in this connection that it was the very same social forces that led to the execution of Jesus and to the condemnation of the thieves. The religious and political authorities approved in each instance. In both cases the same social wisdom was at work to preserve the *status quo*, to maintain in existence the prevailing order of society against disruptive change. Jesus, in his own way, was a threat to established ways of thinking and acting. He threatened the religious order because he broke the law in the name of love. He uncovered the weaknesses of the received traditions and claimed an immediate authority from God. He gained the support of many of the common people who had been discriminated against. He associated with the riffraff of society and brought down upon his head the scorn of the class conscious. So the Scribes and Pharisees and Sadducees took steps to put him down lest he upset the religious establishment.

Jesus was also a threat to the state. It is true that he did not seek to throw off the Roman yoke by military means. The kingdom of which he spoke was of a different sort. Nevertheless, he did have a power over the masses. He was even under suspicion by the Jewish rulers. Wouldn't it be better for the sake of law and order, for peace and security of the land, if he were put down? Pilate apparently thought so. Hence, the evil coalition between religion and politics resulted in the mockery of a trial, a final humiliation, and at last in execution.

In a very profound sense, then, Jesus threatened the established social order just as the thieves did. The difference is that the thieves threatened it because they were worse than most people. Jesus was a threat because he was better than most people. You can get yourself in trouble either way. When Mahatma Gandhi was assassinated George Bernard Shaw remarked, "It just goes to show you how dangerous it is to be good."

These words came to me with a new impact when the word was flashed over the television set that a sniper's bullet had taken the life of Martin Luther King, Jr. The two moral leaders King admired most were Jesus and Gandhi. Like his teachers, he was put to death because he sought to do good. An agitator who stirred up people? Yes! A troublemaker who appealed to the poor and oppressed of the land to seek a new order? Yes! A law breaker who was often in jail? Yes! A revolutionary who threatened the prevailing social order? Yes! But all of this in obedience to the demands of love and the requirements of justice.

Martin Luther King, Jr., was a graduate of Crozer Theological Seminary, where I was later privileged to teach. He was president of the senior class and finished his academic work with a higher grade average than any of his classmates. The Seminary always requests a statement from prospective students regarding their motivation for entering the ministry. When asked why he wanted to become a minister, he wrote, "I felt an inescapable urge to serve society." The urge that led him to wear his body out in behalf of his people was in a real sense the cause of his death. He was carrying out that aim to serve humankind when he was killed. It was symbolic of his life that during his last week on earth he was at work in behalf of the garbage collectors of Memphis. He had a dream, an American dream and a Christian dream, of a land where everybody was free and equal. In pursuit of that idea, he was put in jail. He loved the poor, the outcasts, and the oppressed. Many wanted to kill him. One man did.

When the news was put on the television networks that he was dead, a black woman sat in a bar filled mainly with white men. When they heard the news, they drank a toast and celebrated with cheers. Even the governor of a state could regret his death by violence but then add that he was a troublemaker who caused a lot of turmoil in the land.

During the trouble in Birmingham, King said on one occasion to his black audience something like this, "It may be that a lot more blood will have to be shed on the streets of Birmingham before this thing is over, but let it be our blood and not the blood of our white brothers." And his congregation cheered him and said, "Amen, that's right." For preaching and practicing non-violence, he was hated and despised. For taking Jesus seriously and urging his followers to love their enemies and bless those who cursed them he was called an agitator and a disturber of the peace.

Clarence Jordan was a white man who left his home in Georgia to study theology. He came back from Southern Baptist Theological Seminary with a doctorate in New Testament. That was commendable, everyone thought. But he caused a lot of turmoil when he established an interracial community in Americus, Georgia, several decades ago. He was not very popular with a lot of people for that reason and others. The Koinonia Community farmed on a communal basis. Except for very personal items, they shared the fruits of their labor in common. Eventually, Clarence and some others were ousted from the local Baptist church. To be pacifist, interracial, and to share goods equally seemed strange and even dangerous to those who lived by conventional standards. Yet Clarence and the others were only trying to follow the teachings of the New Testament as they understood them.

One day Clarence and a black man from the community were traveling in a car. They came to a filling station that had only one bathroom, obviously intended for white people. Clarence went to the manager and said, "Would you mind if my brother used your bathroom?" The proprietor seemed a bit puzzled but said, "Why, no, of course not!" When the black man started to the bathroom, he was seen by the manager, who protested, "I thought you said he was your brother." Clarence replied, "He is; he is my brother in

Christ." That is one of the reasons the FBI eventually had to intervene to protect the Koinonia Community from violent attacks.

It is just amazing how people who try to love *everybody* upset the good, decent, law-abiding citizens and church members of this land of ours. I have been reading about a group of social radicals in the South who were active from the time of the Great Depression of the '30s until after Word War II. Most of them were Christians inspired by the example of Jesus and the teachings of the New Testament. Many of them were trained by a social gospel theologian at Vanderbilt University whose name was Alva Taylor. There was H. L. Mitchell of Arkansas who organized the desperately poor tenant farmers. There was Buck Kester of Virginia who was everywhere investigating lynchings, supporting the tenant farmers and sharecroppers, overcoming racial barriers, and all the time defending the poorest people of the land. There was Don West of Georgia who was active in the labor unions in behalf of mill workers and coal miners. All three of these white men, two of them ministers of the gospel, were threatened, run out of town, chased all over the place, and persecuted and hounded by the good, decent people of the country. What was their crime? Loving everybody, defending the poor, organizing desperate and oppressed farmers and laborers, that's all. What was their sin? They tried to get poor white people and poor black people together to fight against the system that kept them down, that's all. That's all they did. And they were persecuted by the good people, the nice, wonderful people who loved their children, read the Bible, went to church, and sometimes drank a little whiskey, and mostly fed their dogs well.

George Bernard Shaw was right. It is dangerous to be good. Socrates illustrates this. Jesus is an example. Gandhi showed that it still holds in modern times. Martin Luther King, Jr., Clarence Jordan, and the radical prophets of the South remind us that it is true in America.

Let us look once more at the three crosses outside Jerusalem. On either side is a thief. In the middle is Jesus. There are two ways to break the law and the conventions of society. You can be worse than most people and break the law from below. Or you can be better than most people and break the law from above. There are two ways to get crucified. One way is to be cruel and violent and hence to be such a menace to society that law-abiding, decent folks take measures to punish you. The other way is to love everybody and seek peace and justice and hence be such a menace to society that law-abiding, decent people take measures to punish you.

If we now return to the Supreme Court decision on segregation and the Watergate era, let us keep these three crosses before us. When people today break the law, they sometimes claim they are acting in pursuit of a great cause that justifies their actions. How shall we respond to this? Violating the law is a serious matter. For individuals to take it upon themselves to decide whether to conform to the demands of society is a dangerous thing. Complex issues arise. Much would need to be said to analyze all that is involved. One thing can be said here. When laws are broken, we have to ask whether the lawbreakers are following in the footsteps of the thieves or following the example of Jesus.

Famous Unknowns
I Have Known

Famous Unknowns

1 Corinthians 1:26-31

My title is an oxymoron. An oxymoron is an expression that appears to be self-contradictory. This past weekend I learned a new oxymoron while visiting with my grandson: "enough toys." As far as Jacob is concerned, there is no such thing as "enough toys." I thought of another oxymoron while I was listening to Dr. Karl Haas' program *Adventures in Good Music*. He was playing pieces composed for the flute. Then he introduced a composition for five flutes written, he said, by an unknown composer whose name he called. This composer was a contemporary of Bach. My logical mind went to work on that. Maybe Dr. Haas meant that this composer was relatively unknown or little known. It seemed oxymoronic to refer to a composer whose name we know and whose music we are hearing as just plain unknown. The incident reminded me of a radio program years ago. It had a segment in which purely fictitious characters were introduced as "famous unknowns." Ah, the composer whose music I was hearing was a famous unknown.

Being practical as well as logical and faced with the necessity of preaching in chapel, I began to wonder if this oxymoron had any homiletical potential. What could be done with "famous unknowns"? The next few minutes will answer that question and perhaps create a new oxymoron — homiletical hope.

It takes but a little imagination to locate some famous unknowns in the Bible. I will mention only one. I refer to the young man mentioned in Mark 14:51. This youth followed Jesus when he was being taken away to trial. He had nothing on but a linen cloth when he was seized. He left the linen cloth and ran away naked. This famous unknown was the original streaker. Who was he?

The writer of Hebrews 11 does a roll call of faith. We are reminded of the famous and not so famous among our spiritual ancestors. The author goes on to speak of the great cloud of witnesses who surround us. Are there not a host of famous unknowns in that cloud? Two thousand years of saints and forgiven sinners since then have been added to the faithful. And what about the famous unknowns still living who labor far and wide in nooks and crannies of Planet Earth to tell the Good News and to show forth the fruits of faith in loving service?

I want to tell you about two famous unknowns that are a part of my memory. The first died in 1990. He was an educated, urban Baptist. The second passed on decades ago. He was an uneducated, rural Baptist.

I got to know Dr. Durward Cason because he was the father of my college roommate. He was a Southern Baptist pastor in the state of Georgia. His more active ministry would have covered the years from about 1925 to about 1975. These five decades were a period of tremendous turmoil and transformation. The relationships between blacks and whites changed for the good. The situation is far from perfect. Compared to the South in which I grew up, things are much better. Just to illustrate the turnaround, do you know the two states with the most segregated public schools? Once it might have been Mississippi, Louisiana, Alabama, or Georgia. According to a radio report I heard, by the early 1980s Illinois was the most segregated. New York was second.

Many forces and many people were responsible for the changes that have taken place in my native Southland. Part of the leaven in that loaf was a white man whose name was Durward Cason. He spent a whole lifetime in the fight against hatred, prejudice, discrimination, and oppression. You did not have to know him very long to understand that this was an urgent concern with him. I regret to say that his passion on the subject put him in a minority among white clergy, but there were others like him.

Let me give you a brief glimpse. One day a black teenage boy came to the front door of his house. Mrs. Cason had just cleaned and waxed the living room floor. It was still wet. So she asked the youth to come around to the back door. When Durward realized what had happened, he was upset and got cross with his wife. She explained to him that the reason she made the request was that the floor was still wet from being cleaned and waxed. She would not let anyone walk on that floor, not even Durward or her own children. She would not have let the Queen of England step on her freshly done floors. Durward understood that. But he was afraid that the teenager would not understand. He would experience that as one more time he was a second-class citizen who could enter the house of a white family only by the back door.

White ministers concerned in those days with breaking down the caste system had some difficult choices to make. One option was to take a bold, aggressive stand in preaching, witness, and action. That approach was likely to get you in trouble with your church. In some cases ministers were asked to leave. The frequent consequence was that someone would be called in his or her place who was conservative on the matter and who could be counted on not to rock the boat.

The other option was to take a cautious approach designed for the long haul. This was in some ways the more difficult road. It required you to be patient, to struggle and suffer with the people. You had to look for every point of possible progress where a little gain, a little growth, a little improvement could be made. It meant biting your tongue when a racist remark was made. It meant hanging on when you wanted to do so much but could accomplish so little. It meant loving people while hating their prejudice. Durward chose this second way.

One of the reasons positive change came to the South with as little violence and bloodshed as occurred was due to the Durward Casons of the region. He was one of the many famous unknowns who made such a witness with integrity and with the slow, agonizing persuasion of suffering love. This is the kind of love that is revealed in the cross of Jesus. Durward was a suffering servant who bore his cross. The work of many Durwards helped prepare the way for change by creating a moral climate in which transformation could take place as a mandate of Christian love and not simply as a requirement of federal law.

There were some famous well-knowns like William Sloan Coffin and Harvey Cox who came down from the North to spend a few days. They got themselves in jail, made their witness, and then went back to the safety of Yale and Harvard. I do not wish to put them down or to belittle their efforts. The public witness of celebrities in focusing public attention on the issue was important. My point is that we ought not to forget the witness of famous unknowns who struggled and suffered and agonized for years and years and years and whose efforts in the end were far more effective.

So I salute you Durward Cason, Servant of Jesus Christ, Agent of the Kingdom, Soldier of the Cross, Famous Unknown. I remember the Casons as the family that welcomed everyone to their front door. And if the floor were dry, Mrs. Cason would let you in.

Now it is time to speak of Old Uncle Wash Oliver. His name was the Reverend Washington Oliver. In the oral tradition of the Friendship Baptist Church community where I grew up, he was always referred to as Old Uncle Wash Oliver. Brother Wash was a country Baptist preacher during the last half of the nineteenth century. He was uneducated. I was told that his wife read his text from the Bible for him before he gave his sermons. According to his tombstone, he baptized at least 5,000 people. I never knew him personally, of course. I did see his picture when I was a child. In an 8x11 incarnation it hung back of the pulpit of Friendship Church. Well, sometimes it hung there. Other times it could be found back in the Sunday school rooms. Some of the good sisters and brothers did not think it was proper for even such a saint as Old Uncle Wash to be in that special place back of the pulpit. Only Jesus deserved that honor. So Brother Wash made many a trip back and forth from the sanctuary to the Sunday school rooms as one faction or the other secretly transported his image to wherever they thought was his proper place.

Uncle Wash, according to tradition, was a fierce prophet who could make sinners tremble. He exhorted them to flee from the wrath to come and to find salvation in the arms of Jesus. Word has it that in the midst of his powerful orations, he sometimes would walk the backs of the benches beseeching sinners to repent and to profess their faith. I don't vouch for the story. I just report the oral tradition.

My favorite story concerns that summer when the drought was so bad. For weeks it had not rained. The hot Georgia sun was wilting the crops and baking the soil. Now and then a cloud would appear, but no relief ever came. For the farmers of the region lack of rain meant disaster. The year's crop of cotton, corn, peanuts, and potatoes was at risk. Without water the crops would die. The people would be in deep trouble. As the dry spell went on, Uncle Wash decided that something had to be done. One morning in church he announced that he would eat no food, drink no water, and would not lie down to sleep until rain came. And with that, he knelt down on his knees and began to pray, beseeching the Almighty to have mercy. And he prayed, and he prayed, and he prayed. I report to you what I was told. About 3:00 in the afternoon clouds began to gather, thunder began to clap, the lightning flashed, and the downpour began. The rain came in gushing torrents. And it kept on coming. The crops were saved. And Old Uncle Wash Oliver sat down to eat his supper.

Some of you may be thinking that Brother Wash had a touch of rheumatism. You suspect that early in the morning he felt a little misery in his bones and figured that the drought was about to end. Maybe so. In all honesty I must admit that in some of my more skeptical moments that thought has crossed my mind. However, on this one I prefer to rest in the New Testament promise that the prayer of the righteous is very effective. In any case, I like to think of Uncle Wash sitting there at his supper table eating his turnip greens and crumbling his corn bread into his buttermilk, listening to the rain still dripping from the trees.

And what does all this have to do with us? It means that for most of us, our destiny is to be a famous unknown. When I think of Durward Cason and Uncle Wash Oliver, I conclude that to be with them among the famous unknowns is a very high calling indeed. Paul reminds the Corinthians that not many of them were wise or powerful or of noble birth. God has chosen the weak and the foolish to be instruments of liberation and reconciliation. If I may paraphrase, God has chosen the famous unknowns of the world to be the primary witnesses of the Word, light of the world, salt of the earth, agents of justice, bearers of love.

Jesus said to those gathered at the Last Judgment that anyone who had showed mercy to the least of these would enter into the joys of the righteous. Did he not also mean that the least of those who showed mercy would inherit everlasting blessedness?

> *Therefore, since we are surrounded by so great a cloud of witnesses, let us also lay aside every weight and sin which clings so closely, and let us run with perseverance the race that is set before us, looking to Jesus the pioneer and perfecter of our faith, who for the joy that was set before him endured the cross, despising the shame, and is seated at the right hand of the throne of God.* — Hebrews 12:1-2

In the cloud of witnesses are the famous whose names everybody knows. Most of the multitude that make up that cloud are famous unknowns recognized only by a few. Durward Cason and Washington Oliver have joined them. In due time, if we keep the faith, you and I will be there. And if you don't mind, I would like to stand by Uncle Wash for a little while. I want to ask him about his rheumatism.

The Good Iranian

Luke 10:25-37

The only time I got a bit scared during the whole episode was when he told me he didn't know the way to the airport. It all started that morning. A pastor who had been in my class that week offered me a ride following the final session on Friday morning. I had been in Morgantown for six days teaching a course for laypeople at West Virginia University. Everything was complete. I was on my way back to Rochester, New York.

The small commuter plane was scheduled to depart at 2:05 p.m. for Pittsburgh. I would change planes for the remainder of the trip. A pastor who had been studying with me all week was driving close to the airport and offered to drop me off. We agreed to leave the dormitory at 1 p.m. Two or three other people also on their way to the airport would join us. At 1:20 p.m. the other passengers had not arrived. My friend said we must leave, else I would miss my plane. As we drove through Morgantown, the pastor's car broke down. The transmission was all locked up. The gears would not change. He jumped out, fooled around a little under the hood, and announced that he would have to find me another ride. The intrepid soul ran right out in the middle of the street and almost forced every car to stop. He told the startled drivers my predicament and begged them to take me to the airport. After a few people had respectfully declined the opportunity, a good-looking young man in a very impressive white sports car stopped, heard the story, and agreed to help.

After my luggage was hastily moved to the new taxi and brief farewells were said, the handsome stranger and I set off. He was quite talkative and chattered away immediately. He was a student at the University from Iran. This was happening in the summer of 1980. American hostages were being held captive by Iranian students. Walter Cronkite was announcing every evening how many days it had been since the crisis began. I was sort of half-way listening. Uppermost in my mind was the fact that the time was passing, and we had a long way to go. I did hear him say that Iranians were not very popular with Americans right now. The way he put it told me that he was unhappy about that. He obviously wanted to be friendly with me. More important on my agenda was that he had made two quick left turns within a couple of blocks. We were now going in the opposite direction from where I thought the airport was. I muttered something to this effect. He replied that he knew another way, a shortcut. Who was I to argue? I knew nothing about the area.

In West Virginia highways usually are going up and down hills or around sharp curves and often both at the same time. They don't call it the "Mountain State" for no reason. We were twisting and turning and zooming through the countryside at speeds exceeding my comfort level. But he appeared to be a good driver. The sports car was one of those expensive luxury models that just loved the kind of death-defying maneuvering we were doing. After a few minutes, it was apparent that we were going farther away from anything remotely resembling an airport. I interrupted his continuing efforts to repair American-Iranian relationships to comment on the fact that we seemed to be going away from the urban scene where we might expect to find large planes arriving and departing. That's when he told me that he didn't know the way to the airport.

It so happened that this was right after one of the hostages had been become ill and was released and sent home. It dawned on me then what the situation was. I was to be the new hostage to replace the departed one. Somewhere nearby in the hills was a helicopter that would transport me to the plane that would take me to Iran. This momentary panic was shortly relieved by what appeared to be genuine remorse on the part of my new friend. He recognized my distress and suggested that we stop and ask for directions. He pulled in at a restaurant. I leaped out, dashed inside, quickly asked for assistance, listened intently, hopped back in the car, and we were off again at breakneck pace. But it wasn't working. We looked for clues that did not appear. At an intersection, he stopped a woman going the opposite direction and asked where the airport was. She pointed us down the same road, so we zoomed on. Still the expected signs were nowhere to be seen. Once again, we pulled off the road and screeched to a halt at a garage. I jumped out and finally located a pair of feet sticking out from under a car. Assuming there were ears at the other end of the body, I blurted out my predicament. From under the car came reassurance that we were proceeding correctly. The faceless voice told me again what I had heard at the restaurant. The newly formed American-Iranian alliance sped down the road.

Finally, as my watch rushed toward 2 p.m., the clues fell into place — the intersection, Route 7, the Kentucky Fried Chicken place, the bank, and a right turn. At last, signs pointing to the airport came into view. Lo and behold, only a few minutes later, we pulled up in front. I thanked my rescuer profusely, heard him stoutly refuse my offer of monetary payment, grabbed my suitcase, and ran inside. As I dashed up to the counter and flashed my ticket, it was just about 2 p.m. The plane was scheduled to depart in less than ten minutes.

Still flushed with my apparent success and the memory of my speedy adventure, I scarcely heard the voice from across the desk saying there was no seat for me. When I recovered enough from the shock to hear the explanation, I learned that the commuter plane had twelve seats. Thirteen confirmed reservations had been issued. I was number thirteen to arrive. I was the odd man out. In my exasperation, I complained that I just had to get back. A wedding rehearsal planned for months was scheduled for that Friday evening in Rochester. I was the minister in charge. The clerk offered to help, grabbed the mike, and announced that a minister was present who needed badly to get on this plane in order to preside over a wedding rehearsal in a few hours. This plane is his last chance of making it. He proceeded to make a lucrative offer to anyone who would surrender a seat and take the next plane. Most of the assembled group looked compassionately at me but offered compelling reasons why their imminent departure was equally urgent, although they would really like to assist.

All seemed lost. Then a woman appeared overflowing with sentiment about how important and beautiful weddings are. She ran on about how important it was for me to get to that rehearsal. She agreed to the seat exchange. I am not sure whether her enthusiasm was motivated by thoughts of weddings, romance, and flowers or whether she just lusted after the money the clerk was offering. Nevertheless, whatever the explanation for her effervescence, the offer was gratefully accepted. Presently, I was sitting crunched up in the crowded little commuter plane. I looked at my watch. It was exactly 2:05 p.m. The rest of the trip was uneventful. I arrived in ample time to greet the happy couple at the wedding rehearsal in Rochester that evening. Let us hope that we all live happily ever after.

Prior to this time I felt no urge to preach on the parable of the Good Samaritan. Don't we already know what this story means? Do we need to hear it again? What more can one add to the obvious truth of the parable about a hated foreigner who gives aid to a stranger in distress? However, this chance encounter with a Good Iranian in West Virginia brought home the truth of this familiar story in a fresh and unexpected way.

We all know that the ancient story begins with one question and ends with another. The lawyer asked, "Who is my neighbor?" Jesus asked, "Who was neighbor to the wounded traveler?" The first question is general, abstract, theoretical, an intellectual adventure in semantics and definition. It is the kind of question one might expect from a lawyer or a theologian. These are professions noted for their proclivities for precise statement and frequent distinctions. The lawyer's question was, above all, safe, non-involving, and non-threatening, an issue for a seminar discussion. The lawyer raised the point anyway to test Jesus. If you are so smart, if you have wisdom from on high, tell me what you mean when you speak of loving a neighbor. Who is my neighbor anyway? That's a complicated question, you know.

The question that Jesus put at the end is practical, particular, concrete, about real life as it is lived on streets and highways. It is personally involving, particularly after what has gone before. Who was neighbor to the man who fell into the hands of a criminal? The priest, the Levite, or the Samaritan? This brings the issue down to specifics. It calls for a decision about a particular event. Now it is the lawyer who is being put to the test.

Then there is the element of surprise and shock. Who is the hero in this story? The answer is unexpected. The good person is neither the priest nor the Levite. The one who was neighbor is not the one who might be expected to receive commendation. The center of attention is not even on a member of the favored race, not even one of the elect whom God has chosen for a special destiny. The hero is not a Jew but a Samaritan, a member of a despised group. This story cuts through prejudice and cliche and the untested assumptions by which so much of life is lived. The question Jesus posed goes right to the heart of the matter. Who is my neighbor? Anyone in need, any specific person in a given set of circumstances who is in distress. Who is neighbor? A neighbor is one who shows mercy to somebody in trouble. This story reduces life to fundamental, simple truths, unencumbered by the complications and obscurities with which religion often overlays the basics.

All of this came home to me in a vivid and unexpected way as I, anxious and sweating, zoomed up the hills, around the curves, and down into the valleys of West Virginia with a stranger from a foreign country. Looking back on it, I think our chance encounter went through three stages in about 25 minutes.

First of all, we confronted each other as an American and an Iranian. Our talk turned to politics and international relations. He remarked that Americans don't like Iranians right now. He saw me as one of those Americans and wondered if I liked Iranians. I saw him as a foreigner whose nation held my fellow-Americans captive. We were both suspicious and anxious, wondering what the other felt, what the American thought about Iranians and what the Iranian thought about Americans.

In a second move, we came to see each other as just two people. He came to see my distress. I needed to get to the airport. His whole attitude changed when he admitted he didn't know where the airport was and then saw the anxiety and puzzlement that spread across my face when that news struck me. I came to see him as an individual human being who had a genuine desire for friendship. That's he why he talked so much. That's why he offered to go out of his way, to take his own personal time, and to drive me — a total stranger — to meet my plane. At first he had been so intent on talking and establishing contact with me that the airport was not really in his mind. Initially, I had been so focused on getting there on time that I was impatient with his chatter.

It all changed out on the highway when his agenda became my agenda, and my agenda became his. He was sorry he had not taken my need seriously and had driven aimlessly around talking about politics and international affairs. I was sorry I had been so suspicious of him and had not heard his plea for some sign of friendship. Then we became partners involved in a common enterprise of finding the airport. In the next few minutes we came to be neighbors to each other. From that moment on it didn't matter that one human being was an Iranian and the other human being was an American. We were just two people out on a road in the West Virginia hills, who for those few minutes needed each other.

We were thrown together by chance circumstances like that Jewish traveler and that Good Samaritan who happened to come along. I have since wondered if, as they journeyed down the road to the hotel, that Samaritan turned to that Jew and said, "You know, Jews don't like Samaritans much right now."

We reached a third stage in our encounter on the airport road. We rode that final distance to the airport as this specific Iranian and this individual American. We cannot fully abstract our humanity from the fact that we are certain kinds of human beings. We are white, black, Jew, Samaritan, male, female, Russian, Chinese, Protestant, Catholic, Christian, Muslim, and so on and on. These particularities make us what we, as individuals, are as human beings. Anyone who hears me preach knows as soon as I speak that I am from the South. That fact is important. It shapes and molds me in a thousand ways beyond the fact that I sound funny to Yankees who sound funny to me.

When the lawyer asked for a definition of neighbor, Jesus did not expound on humanity. He did not offer generalization about how we are all just people. He told a story about two human beings on the Jericho road, one a Jew and the other a Samaritan. This particularity is crucial to the story. When we arrived at the airport, the fact was that our chance encounter as two human beings on the Morgantown road took on its distinctive and peculiar meaning because he was an Iranian and I was an American.

On a highway in Morgantown, West Virginia, I relearned the lesson Jesus taught a long time ago about a Samaritan and a Jew. For one brief moment an American and an Iranian were able to get past the headlines that put our nations at odds with one another. For a short time we reached out to each other as two human beings who needed a friend then and there. I needed a ride to the airport. He needed someone to see him as an individual and to be nice to him. I probably will never hear the parable of the Good Samaritan ever again without thinking of that up and down and around and around road to the airport and of the Good Iranian who was neighbor to an American.

The Amazing Dr. Hobbs —
And The Other Side Of The Story

James 5:13-18

"I don't know how the universe works. I don't understand the great mysteries. All I know is that we prayed for Eric, and he is better." So said the amazing man as he stood in my office on the third floor staring intently out the window. Cecil Hobbs graduated from Colgate-Rochester Divinity School in 1933. He had been a student when the seminary moved from its downtown location to a new campus on the south side of the city. Cecil told me that he helped plant and tend the grass that grew all around the building. He had since served as a missionary teacher in Burma and as an Asian specialist for many years in the Library of Congress. More recently he had served churches in the Washington, D.C., area. I came to know him when he returned to Rochester to work on his Doctor of Ministry degree. His dissertation dealt with the reality and power of prayer. But the astonishing thing was how he lived out his thesis in life. Cecil was a man of prayer. His written work is vibrant with faith and insight into the meaning of communion with God. He was living testimony to depths of the spirit that most of us have not found.

It was the first day of a summer school class in Prayer, Providence, and the Problem of Evil — a heavy topic for warm days. We spent some time introducing ourselves to each other. I asked the students to tell me why they were interested in the topic. One woman said, "I am Ann Klein. I was supposed to be in Sweden visiting relatives. But a few days ago I took my son to R Wing of Strong Hospital." She explained that R Wing is the psychiatric unit. Then she concluded, "Since I have to be in Rochester anyway, I thought a class on Prayer, Providence, and the Problem of Evil might be appropriate. So here I am." The Reverend Cecil Hobbs was also in that class. He introduced himself and told of his lifelong interest in the meaning of prayer. He also told us how much prayer had meant in his own personal life.

Afterward Cecil sought Ann and asked what her son's name was. Told that it was Eric, Cecil said that he would pray for him. A few days after that in class someone quoted a prominent theologian to the effect that prayer without personal commitment is not worth much. That struck Cecil as right to the point. He went home and told his wife Cecile about the class. "Here I have been praying for Eric. But if I am really serious, I have to back that up with some action. I know now I must go see him." That's what he did. He located Eric in R Wing of the hospital watching television. Putting out his hand, he said, "I'm Cecil Hobbs. I'm in a class with your mother. Could we talk?" Eric agreed. Cecil asked him if he prayed and was told, "Not much." But he was willing to have Cecil pray for him. So they engaged in a season of quietness in which Cecil asked God to help Eric find balance and wholeness in his life. This happened on a Wednesday afternoon.

One morning Cecil and Cecile met Ann coming into the main building of the seminary on the way to my class. Cecil proposed that they go into the library and pray for Eric. It was early in the day. No one else was present. I am sure that many times prayer has emanated from that reading room as students prepared for exams. "O Lord of Hosts, be with us yet. Lest we forget, lest we forget." But I doubt if those walls had ever seen anything quite like this. The three of them formed a circle of hands. Cecil led them in prayer. Right out loud in the library where quietness is the first rule, he offered thanks to God and lifted up Eric to the mercies of the Almighty.

Ann kept me up to date with all this. She had never met anyone quite like Cecil. She told me how much it meant to her that someone she had never met before had shown such interest in her and in her son. She was amazed. It didn't take long before you felt like you had known Cecil all your life. He soon became your friend.

What we all noticed was that whenever Cecil was around, you prayed. And you were glad. It was always better afterwards. She was so grateful that Cecil had taken the time to go to the hospital to visit Eric and to pray with him. She reported to me that Eric was better. She asked the doctor when the improvement was first noted. He said that as he recalled, Eric had been different since Wednesday afternoon. Wasn't that the day Cecil had been there?

Cecil came into my office one day. We talked about Eric, the class, prayer, and other things. Cecil stood in the middle of the room. He got a very serious look on his face. He looked pensively out the window. From my office on the third floor of a building on top of a hill, the surrounding suburbs and the outlying countryside can be seen. My office is situated so that I had the best view that can be had from those heights. The most impressive thing is that on a clear day the Bristol Hills come into view about thirty miles away. Cecil looked hard at those mountains. I am pretty sure they trembled a little as my friend put them under his scrutiny. Up to that time I had always taken that verse about faith moving mountains with a grain of salt. That was a bit of Oriental hyperbole, we all said. Now I am not so certain.

"Professor Cauthen," he began. I could never persuade him to call me by my first name, as students half my age and one third his do routinely. I was his "mentor," and he felt better calling me by my title. Cecil was a gentleman and a scholar of the old school. I was not used to that kind of deference. Anyway, he went on. "I don't understand how the universe works. I don't understand the great mysteries. All I know is that we prayed for Eric, and he is better." How could one fail to think of that passage in James on such an occasion: "Therefore confess your sins to one another, and pray for one another, that you may be healed. The prayer of a righteous man has great power in its effects" (James 5:16). So the term moved on toward its end. Exams were taken; papers were handed in. The class was over.

All too quickly it was time for Cecil and Cecile to return to their home in Virginia. He came in to see me and to talk about work on his thesis. He wanted to set forth his convictions about prayer. We made plans for keeping in touch and for getting his committee together. It was also the day we had to say good-bye for the time being. When it was time for him to leave, he came over to my desk. "I want us to pray," he said. A visit with Cecil would not be complete without prayer. It never seemed awkward or forced. It was the most natural thing in the world to talk to God when he was around. Cecil had a way about him that made God a partner in every conversation. And you were glad Cecil was there, because he always knew just what to say to God. The world always felt a little friendlier somehow.

Cecil stood by me as I sat at my desk. He took my hand and held it in a firm grip. Then he prayed in words something like this. "O Lord, our Creator, we thank you for the new friends we have made this summer. And we thank you for Professor Cauthen here and for the work he does. Bless him as he works with his students preparing them to go out into the world to preach the gospel and to carry on their ministry. Help him to do a good job. Watch over him and keep him...." The prayer ended. Cecil was gone. I was left with misty eyes but with a more cheerful and optimistic outlook on things. That moment of prayer lifted my spirits for the day.

He came back for his graduation to receive the D. Min. degree. He brought me a lovely picture of the seminary campus taken in winter. It was made by his daughter. I cherish it both for its beauty and for the memories it brings of Cecil. I spent the night at his house on my way to Georgia a few summers ago. Cecile was now in a nursing home, and we went to visit her. Some time after that he joined his wife in the nursing home. He remained healthy and active for a long time. He walked, spent time writing, and did all the right things when it came to diet and exercise. He worked on a book that recorded his life and his thoughts about things. You can be sure that prayer figured prominently in his reflections. His letters were always welcome. Sometimes he included a prayer or a poem he had written. I used one of his prayers in a worship service that he had sent me a few days earlier. It was vintage Hobbs. His letters were always upbeat. He always told me that he was thinking of me and always sent greetings and good wishes to my wife. He would always bring me up to date on what he and Cecile had been doing and thinking. Any day the phone might ring. On the other end would be his strong voice with a word of greeting and encouragement. I was only one of many who were blessed with his continuing ministry of letters and phone calls. He was indeed the amazing Dr. Hobbs. I use the past tense now because one day came a note from his daughter that Cecil has passed on. It was only a matter of days when another letter came saying that Cecile had joined him in death. An era in my life had come to an end.

I used to stand my office now and then and look out the window. I would pause for a few moments thinking and surveying the countryside. Sometimes I recalled that this was the window that Cecil stared through when he fixed the Bristol Hills in his gaze. He confessed that he didn't know much about how the universe worked. He just knew that we prayed for Eric, and Eric got better. I thought about all these things and remembered with gratitude my friendship with Cecil. I can still feel the firm grip of his hand on mine as he asked God to bless his mentor, his professor, and his friend. Then I would look closely at the Bristol Hills. Didn't they used to be a little farther over to the left? Anyway they have never been quite the same since Cecil looked at them as he pondered the power of prayer.

This would be a good place to bring this sermon to a conclusion. Here it is all wrapped up with a nice little touch at the end. But it cannot end yet. I'll tell you why. I told the story about Cecil and Eric and Ann in a sermon one day in a church in Rochester. The people liked it. At least they said they did as they walked past. Of course, I was blocking the exit. There was no way to get out without passing me. Saying a good word seemed the best way to get past. One woman told me they were beginning a series on prayer in her study group. The sermon would be a good way to begin, she said. She was grateful for the story about the amazing Dr. Hobbs. When everyone had departed, I was feeling pretty good about the service. I walked back into the sanctuary to retrieve my Bible and my notes.

A woman was waiting for me at the front of the church. She was crying. She asked if she could talk to me. I said, of course. She told me that she had a son much like Eric. When he was sick, many people prayed for him. They prayed and prayed. But he got no better. He never did. With that experience in her mind, she did not know quite what to do with my sermon. Could I help her? It had seemed like such a good day up to this point. Why did it have to get spoiled like this? I don't remember exactly what I said. I stumbled for words. I did comment that she had told the other side of the story. That side has to be taken into account too. We talked for a while, and we both left the church.

So when you recall the story of the amazing Dr. Hobbs, don't forget the other side of the story. But when you remember the other side of the story, don't forget the amazing Dr. Hobbs. I still think that when Cecil fixed them in his gaze, the Bristol Hills trembled a little.

The Deacons And The Demons

Ephesians 6:10-20

"I don't care what the Bible says." He spoke in anger and exasperation. Still it was disturbing to hear a deacon in a Baptist church say these words. He, of course, did care — he cared a lot. He was driven to this outburst by the frustration he felt. He had come to tell me that the deacons wanted to have a meeting. He refused to call it without inviting me. It seems that some of the brothers wanted to remove me from the pastorate of the church I had served for nearly two years. The integrity of the chairman of the Board of Deacons would not allow a gathering in my absence. With heavy heart he had come to tell me the purpose of the meeting and to invite me to be present. The uproar had come about because I had written some letters to the newspapers and had preached a sermon that marked me as an integrationist. This was not a popular position in the prevailing climate in the deep South. The surrounding issue was the 1954 decision of the Supreme Court outlawing segregation in the public schools.

When the chairman advised me of the movement to have me ousted, a long and fruitless argument ensued. We argued about the wisdom of what I had done in my letters and in the more recent sermon. The greater offense, according to him, was the letters. They advertised to the world that a deviant thinker occupied the pulpit in this little town. It put the membership in a bad light, he said. I defended myself by an appeal to Scripture. "Show me on the basis of the Bible that I am wrong," I remonstrated, "and I will take it all back." I thought this would clinch the argument, or at least shift attention away from me to exegesis of the Book. Was I ever wrong!

For it was then that this good deacon startled me by saying, "I don't care what the Bible says; we are not going to permit our schools to be integrated!"

This was a good man, a faithful Christian, admired and held in high esteem by everyone in that little town. He was the sort of person you would like to have as a neighbor. He would go out of his way to help you, regardless of your color. He was kind, considerate, friendly, and generous to a fault. He was old enough to be my father. I knew he loved me like a son. And I loved him. When it came to his attention that I had used a lot of gasoline doing my pastoral visitation to the sick in the community and in the Atlanta hospitals, he would quietly call me aside and invite me to stop by the station he ran for a free fill-up. Above all his integrity was beyond question. He was chairman of the deacons. He believed the Holy Word of God with all his heart. Yet here he was saying to the preacher who had angered him, "I don't care what the Bible says!"[1]

I met with the deacons on the following Saturday night. It was a tense situation and feelings were deep. We were all nervous and uneasy. At first I thought my service as pastor was soon to end. Then things took a turn in the opposite direction. First, it came to light that some of the rumors flying around were false. In my hometown twenty miles away, it was being circulated that during my infamous sermon, everyone in the church stood up and marched right out the door. The deacons at that meeting knew that only one person had departed. He was not even a church member or a local resident. More important was the fact that it was being spread around that everyone who had invited the guest revivalist due in next week and me to supper had cancelled their invitations. One deacon said, "Well, they are supposed to come to my house, and I am still expecting them."

The crucial statement was made by an older man. He too was a pillar of the church and community, a good man, a solid rock of character and rectitude. He along with some of the others were three of the finest men in the state of Georgia, bar none. I would have trusted my life in the hands of either one of them, even that night! One of them spoke up after the meeting had gone on for some time. He said something to this effect: "I am mad, too. I don't like what the preacher has done any more than the rest of you. But as long as he is my pastor, I will stand by his side and defend his right to preach his conscience. This is a Baptist church. We have to keep the pulpit free. Who would want to come and be our pastor when the word got around that we threw this man out because we didn't like what he said?"

It was a magnificent statement by a loyal church member whose Baptist theology ran as true and deep as the furrows this man of the soil plowed in his cotton fields. He was angry with me, but I was his pastor. He would not turn against me now, no matter what everybody else might do. I shall never forget the character and strength he displayed that night. That statement carried weight. His defense defined the tone and outcome of the meeting from that point on. I stayed on in the church for a while longer until I left to enter the graduate school of Vanderbilt University in the fall of 1955.

The oldest of these men have all gone to their reward since then. When I go back to visit that little town, I like to walk through the cemetery and stand by the grave of each one of them. I pause to remember the night they stood by my side. Even though they were upset that I had disturbed the peace with my unpopular racial views, they spoke up for me. They were men of integrity and faith, loyal to their young pastor even in their anger and dismay.

What are we to do with what that deacon blurted out in my living room? "I don't care what the Bible says!" Others might in a moment of irritation under the same circumstances have come out with the same thing. Neither one, of course, could have lived with such a principle for very long. Their faith and their honesty were too real for that. They were Baptists, after all, and good ones too. These honorable deacons were caught up in deep conflict. On the one hand was their cultural inheritance ingrained in them since their mothers fed them at their breasts. On the other hand was their loyalty to me as the pastor they loved and their belief in the freedom of the pulpit.

They were puzzled by my deviation from the cultural norms that other pastors had honored. I am sure that in all the many years these men had sat in the pews of that church, no preacher had ever before challenged the segregation of the races as morally offensive. What were they to do with this young upstart who had offered this novel proposition and made the stakes very high by claiming to do so in the name of biblical justice and Christian love? Something had to give. In his animosity and indignation in that tense moment, this good deacon let go one set of his convictions in order to honor the other. A battle raged within his heart. At one moment, he said out loud that he was willing to give up his allegiance to God's own Word in order to be a good white man of Georgia. In the long run, I knew, and perhaps he knew too, that if he really were persuaded that the Good Book were against him, he would have to change his outlook on life. I knew where his ultimate loyalty was.

I watched my own father as the same battle went on in his heart. The turning point came when he attended my graduation from Yale Divinity School. It was his first trip north of the state of Georgia. About 100 classmates of mine assembled to receive the degree we had earned. In my class were men and (a few) women from all over the world — from Asia, Africa, Europe, and from most of the states in the Union. Yellow, white, and black, we received the same degree. We were given the same commission to go forth into the world to preach the gospel. Reflecting upon the meaning of that occasion for him, my father later said to me in the idiom of his own Baptist piety something like this: "You know, it occurred to me that if we are to be together in heaven when we die, we had better start learning to live together down here." That's pretty good theology. That occasion marked a new beginning for him. After that, he tried to live by the principle that all are equally precious in God's sight. I knew that he often quietly urged his black friends to get everybody registered to vote. That was the way to make the politicians take notice.

Those deacons were of the same cast of mind and sentiment as my father. I don't know where they stood on racial matters by the time they were called away from this world. Maybe they never underwent the conversion my dad did. Maybe they didn't have a son to urge them gently on. I do believe that had the right life experiences been available to them, they would have given up their prejudices before they would renounce the Holy Scriptures. Their Baptist faith and their Christian goodness were far too deep for it to be otherwise.

The theologian in me wants to probe a bit more the inner conflict that raged in their souls. The author of Ephesians provides the clue we need. The writer uses the imagery of battle between opposing forces to interpret situations like this. He urges believers to put on the whole armor of God in order to resist the wiles of the devil. Then comes the crucial insight. "For we are not contending against flesh and blood, but against the principalities, against the powers, against the world rulers of this present darkness, against the spiritual hosts of wickedness in the heavenly places" (Ephesians 6:12). For modern ears, the notion that bad spirits inhabit the heavens and do mischief on earth is strange. What can it mean for us?

I translate this reference to demonic powers into another idiom. The spiritual hosts of wickedness are destructive powers from the past living on to produce moral blindness that results in suffering and injustice. What we wrestle against is not bad invisible beings, not literal devils. Rather in this world we are enslaved by the continuing influence of those historical developments that created a society based on racial domination. The creators of this order invented an ideology to make it sound good, to give it moral status. Those three deacons were inhabited by demonic influences. They did not invent those evil ideas and practices but inherited them along with the accent in their speech. The demonic power lived on as they appropriated the past and embraced these unjust ideas and institutions as their own. They did so not knowing how evil the system was, even though the evidence was plain for all to see. They did so not knowing they were being deceived, not realizing that what they accepted as good was demonic.

Slavery and segregation could not survive if they were thought to be wrong. White church and white state and white society were all seduced by the lie that one race is better than another. In effect all conspired to promote the evil while calling it good. The power of these forces from the past was as real as literal devils. Moral blindness is a disease passed silently on from generation to generation. At last it afflicted these three decent men. They defended segregation under the illusion that they were innocent in doing so. So deeply enslaved were they by the evil powers that one of their number could say, "I don't care what the Bible says." That was the biggest lie of all.

What was going on in the heart of the Baptist deacon who uttered those words that contradicted his own deepest convictions? My suggestion is that the demonic was at work in the guise of the destructive power of the past that blinded him. He was beguiled by the influence of a culture that could not see beyond the ideology of race to the truth that unites all human beings as the children of God for whom Christ died.

In chapter 2, the author of Ephesians points to the liberating might of Christ who breaks down the walls of partition between the estranged so that reconciliation and peace can reign in the world. Christ conquers the demons, overcomes the lies, opens eyes to truth, releases hearts from evil prejudices, so that light and love might prevail. What does this ancient language mean? How does the gospel free us from the principalities that inhabit the heavenly places? How does Christ liberate us from the demonic powers? He does so, I believe, by awakening us to the deeper truth that slumbers within us and by making effective in us the power of color-blind love that unites all human beings under God.

The Bible that this good Baptist temporarily disavowed teaches that we are to love our neighbor as we love ourselves. Our neighbor is any close-by person regardless of race, religion, or creed. The Bible deeply ingested leads us toward forms of social life in which all have equal claims to the means to fulfillment. However, it takes some life experience to move these truths from the head into the heart. Only then will the inherited cultural demons be cast out so that the awakening to truth can become effective in practice.

One of my experiences came early when I observed that my friend Ben, Jr., who was black, walked to school three miles. I rode on a bus to a better-equipped institution. It puzzled me that no one else seemed to be bothered by this obvious discrepancy. After all, the professed philosophy even under segregation was "separate but equal." The practice was "separate and unequal." Everybody knew it. Yet the good white people continued to mouth the hypocrisy of segregated equality. Most of them were church members. My father's awakening came at my graduation from seminary. The truth about race is so transparent that once the blinders are removed, you wonder why you didn't see it all along. The demons cause the blindness. It makes the evil appear to be good.

I don't know if those honorable deacons ever underwent the transforming experience or not. It would have been a liberating new birth for them if it did happen. They would be glad it came about. Then they would no longer have that contradiction in their soul. Then they could sing that old song they loved so well with new meaning and gratitude. "Amazing Grace, that saved a wretch like me. Once I was blind but now I see." They would rejoice to be free from the demonic power that once made one of them say to his pastor, "I don't care what the Bible says."

---

1. The preceding paragraphs were originally published in *The Many Faces Of Evil*, CSS Publishing Co., Lima, Ohio, 1997, pp. 79-80. Used by permission.

Communion

Risking Spirit

1 Corinthians 11:23-26; Mark 14:22-26

A Communion Meditation
He had almost committed suicide at this very spot. Now he was glad he didn't. Robert Frost was strolling along the seashore near Kitty Hawk, North Carolina. As he walks on the sands, he recalls that sixty years ago he came to this same place in a moment of despondency. Elinor White, his girlfriend, had refused him. He came here to kill himself. He would make her sorry by walking into the nearby swamp and disappearing without a trace. At the edge of the swamp, however, he came upon some hunters who took him back to safety in Elizabeth City. Sixty years later he was again at Kitty Hawk. Now he was a huge success. He was in effect the poet laureate of the nation.

He thought about his own desperate failure in the past and now the astounding success. He recalled that the sands of Kitty Hawk had witnessed other failures and other successes. It was near here that the first English colony was planted on American soil. It was planted in vain. All the settlers perished. Another failure had taken place just off the shore. Aaron Burr's daughter, Theodosia, was aboard a vessel that had set out from Charleston, South Carolina. She was going to meet her father who was returning from a four-year self-imposed exile in Europe. A storm off Hatteras upset the boat. All were drowned, including Theodosia. But Kitty Hawk was also the place where the Wright brothers made their first successful flight in an airplane.

As Frost thought about this, he saw that history is not simply a series of failures and successes. More important was the way the human spirit takes risks and makes heroic efforts. Then the light flashed in his mind. Insight dawned, and he wrote these lines:

> *Then I saw it all.*
> *God's own descent*
> *into flesh was meant*
> *as a demonstration*
> *that the supreme merit*
> *lay in risking spirit*
> *in substantiation.*

These lines appear in a poem called "Kitty Hawk." It came to my attention one spring some years ago. March and April bring, among other things, a batch of dissertations from doctoral students hoping to receive their degrees in May. One of them, surprisingly enough, provides the inspiration for this communion meditation. The thesis dealt with the religious implications of the poetry of Robert Frost. One poem struck me as particularly appropriate as we sit around the Lord's Table to celebrate our life as Christians.

In these lines from "Kitty Hawk," Frost says that the incarnation of God in Jesus was a demonstration of supreme merit. It was spirit taking risk in becoming vulnerable in human flesh. God had risked all in order to be present to humanity. It was a risk that ended on a cross. In a flash, Frost says, he saw it all. The meaning of life is to be found in risk taking, in heroic efforts to achieve. Some risks end in failure; some end in success. Some result in disaster in the beginning but victory in the long run. History is the story of crucifixion and resurrection, of suffering and triumph.

God's noblest act was to swoop down to humankind. The noblest act of humanity would be to soar toward God as the Wright brothers rose toward the heavens. Both the movement of God toward us and of us toward God is a demonstration that the supreme merit lies in risking spirit seeking incarnation in deeds.

As we gather around the Lord's Table, the great realities of the Christian life come to mind. Faith, hope, love — these three all represent spirit reaching out, risking. Consider faith. Jesus said that as we eat this bread, we should be reminded of his body that was broken for us in demonstration of God's love. This event in the past is the basis for our faith. We remember this revelation of divine love, and we believe. *Faith is spirit taking risk.* It is not always easy to believe that God is love. Much of life seems to teach otherwise. History often appears to speak as much of chaos and of divine indifference as it does of God's benevolence and caring.

We look not only to the past in remembrance of the basis of our faith. We look also to the future in hope. Jesus said that as often as we eat this bread and drink this cup, we would proclaim his death until he comes again. *Hope is spirit taking risk.* It is confidence in a victory that is still to come. Hope is not yet the reality. We hope for what we do not see. Will the masses of the poor ever have food? Will the oppressed and the outcasts ever know justice? Will the nations learn to live in peace? Will refugees ever find a home? Will those who are lonely ever find a friend? Will pain and sorrow ever end? Hope is confidence that victory will come when it is still not yet in sight. Hope is confidence tinged with uncertainty. Hope is spirit risking toward the future.

We live not only by faith and in hope; we seek to live in love here and now with one another. *Love is spirit taking risk.* If we reach out to others, they may not respond. If we go the second mile, those whose burdens we assume may not show gratitude. Love risks rejection. Jesus was the embodiment of perfect love; his life ended on a cross.

Faith, hope, love — these are the realities we celebrate at the Lord's Table. It is only in taking the risk of faith that we shall ever find truth. It is only in taking the risk of hope that we can ever find victory over evil. It is only in taking the risk of love that reconciliation can ever be real. It was only in spirit risking substantiation in the flesh of Jesus that salvation became possible. It is only in spirit reaching out to receive Christ in faith, hope, and love that salvation can ever be real.

As we gather around this communion table, let us come seeking nourishment and refreshment and a renewal of faith, hope, and love — spirit taking risk reaching out to God and to each other.

Memories, Memories, Memories

1 Corinthians 11:23-26

Reflections For Maundy Thursday

Memories, memories — how important they are to our lives! If you are as old as I am, you probably remember where you were and what you were doing on December 7, 1941. On that day the Japanese bombed Pearl Harbor. I was in the living room that Sunday afternoon in my home in Griffin, Georgia. I was eleven years old. One of my parents picked up the phone and heard a voice telling someone to turn on the radio. We were all on party lines in those days. So we turned on the radio and heard the news about the attack.

That Sunday night we went to church with another family. As we were driving back from Bethel Baptist Church, which was out in the country, we saw a big red glow in the sky toward Griffin. Our momentary thought was that the Japanese had already bombed our own little hometown. But sanity returned soon, and we dismissed that rather far-fetched possibility. It turned out that the dressing rooms at the swimming pool had caught fire and burned. The next day I and other seventh graders of Orr's Grammar School gathered around a radio to hear President Roosevelt speak of the "day that will live in infamy." He asked Congress to declare war on Japan.

I remember also the day President Roosevelt died. We all asked, "Who is Harry Truman? How can he possibly take Roosevelt's place?" That afternoon my best friend Charlie Perkins walked about three miles from his house to mine to talk about it. We all went to prayer meeting that night.

I remember as well the day the troops landed on Normandy, the day the Germans surrendered, the days the atomic bombs were dropped on Hiroshima and Nagasaki, and when the Japanese surrendered. All these things were many years ago. Yet they live on in that treasury we call our memory. Memories, memories, memories — how important they are to our lives.

It seems that most of the national events we remember in the '60s were bad. We remember where we were and what we were doing when President John Kennedy was assassinated, when Senator Robert Kennedy was shot, and when Dr. Martin Luther King, Jr., was killed. When the last event occurred, my daughter Nancy was seven years old. We lived in Wilmington, Delaware. She had seen her mother and father crying that day when we heard that he had been killed. There were rumors of riots in the big cities. Nancy was confused about what it all meant. That night I went up with her to tell her a goodnight story. She said to me, "Daddy, why would anyone want to shoot Dr. King?" I shall never forget that question. Why indeed? Racism was a word and a reality Nancy didn't know about.

This was the little girl who had been in the car the night we saw *Guess Who's Coming to Dinner* at the drive-in. When the young white woman brought her black fiancé home, her mother's mouth dropped open when she first saw them. Nancy saw the mother's shock and did not understand. She said, "What's the matter?" That's how innocent Nancy was of racism. That's why she asked me, "Daddy, why would anyone want to shoot Dr. King?" I was at a loss for words. I tried to explain that some people didn't like him, thought he was a troublemaker. Some people even hated him. That's why someone shot him. Memories, memories, memories — how important they are to our lives!

There was one good recollection from that decade. I would guess that many of you stayed up late that summer night in July 1969, when Neil Armstrong stepped onto the surface of the moon. What an exciting moment that was. For a little while it helped take our minds off Vietnam and all the trouble, confusion, and turmoil of those years. Memories, memories, memories — how important they are to our lives!

Nothing is more essential to making us human than the power to bring to mind what happened once upon a time. The past lives on in our ability to recall those events that have made us who we are as individuals and as a people. If memory were lost, we would cease to be the persons we are. We would have no identity, no sense of where we belong in the scheme of things.

Nations have memories. Every year on the Fourth of July, we celebrate the birth of our independence. We recall those documents that say who we are as Americans. We use the occasion to remind ourselves once more where we came from, to ask if we have been true to the ideals of freedom, equality, and justice for all. We live by appropriating the past, reinterpreting its meaning for today, and creating our own new meanings in preparation for tomorrow. Without a past, we have no present identity and no direction for the future. Memories, memories — how important they are to our lives!

Individuals and families have memories. What an interesting time we could have if just went around calling up those important occasions from times past. Parents remember the day each of their children was born. The night Paul, my oldest child, came into this world, Eloise had been scheduled to attend a shower given by her Sunday school class. Paul arrived two weeks earlier than expected. I stayed with Eloise until early evening. Then I left Vanderbilt University Hospital in Nashville, Tennessee, for the shower. There I was, the only man present. When the time came, I began to open the gifts. One item was a mystery to me. I held it up and exclaimed over it. "How nice, how cute!" The problem was that I was holding it upside down. The women had a good laugh at my expense. Memories, memories, memories — how important they are to our lives!

We recall those significant times of passage in particular — births, graduations, new jobs, marriages, the serious illnesses, and the crises that turned out well and those that did not. We like to remember the good times. Eighteen years after he arrived in this world in Nashville, Tennessee, Paul was a senior in high school in Brighton High School in New York. He had applied to a dual degree program at Oberlin College and at the Oberlin Conservatory of Music. It was April 15. He had not heard from his application. He called me at school to tell me that the mail had arrived. Nothing had come from Oberlin. I suggested that he call the college and inquire. "After all," I said, "they promised to let you know by April 15." A few minutes later the phone rang again. I picked it up to hear a very excited voice exclaim, "Dad, I was accepted into both." Good news for Paul and for the whole family that day. Memories, memories, memories — how important they are to our lives!

We remember the not-so-happy times as well. In 1966-67 I was on sabbatical leave in Chicago. Nancy was in the first grade. One spring day Eloise was measuring Nancy for a new dress. "Stand up straight," her mother said. "I am standing up straight, Mommy," was the reply. That brought to our attention that Nancy had a curved spine. For the next dozen years scoliosis would be a familiar word in our family. Fortunately, we lived in Delaware near the Dupont Institute, a center of advanced research and treatment for scoliosis. We received a great deal of free care of the highest sort, made possible by large gifts from the Dupont family. For Nancy this meant first wearing an upper body cast all the time, then a Milwaukee brace for 23 hours a day. For a decade she spent her daily life encased in steel and leather. She was the object of attention and crude remarks by thoughtless kids. Eventually her spine was essentially straight. I shudder to think what her life might have been like before the advent of modern medicine and technology. Memories, memories, memories — how important they are to our lives.

And we remember the dying too. On October 21, 1987, the mother of Paul, Nancy, and Melissa passed away at age 55. For years she had fought it with surgery, chemotherapy, and the best that doctors had to offer. Finally, the cancer got to her liver. Then it was just a matter of time. She spent her last months in the wonderful care of volunteers at Mt. Carmel Hospice in Rochester. Gradually the disease worked its evil. At 11:55 a.m., the nurse took away her stethoscope and stepped back from the bed. We knew the end had come mercifully to release her from her suffering. Memories, memories — how important they are to our lives!

Religious communities also have memories. The house of Israel remembered above all else those days in Egypt under Pharaoh's bondage. They recalled the coming of Moses, the Exodus, the wandering in the wilderness, and the making of covenant with Yahweh, their God. It was these crucial events that constituted them as a people. They defined their identity, marked their destiny, and formed the common bond by which they were united to all other Jews.

We Christians have memories too. We come here this evening to recall the night on which Jesus was betrayed. Tomorrow we will remember the cross. On Sunday we will remember and celebrate the resurrection of Christ from the dead. These are the crucial events that define us as a community of Christian believers. We know who we are because of what we remember. So we gather here tonight to tell once again the old, old story of Jesus and his love, to confess that Jesus Christ is the church's one foundation, to recall the old rugged cross, to survey the wondrous cross on which the Prince of glory died. We assemble to remember that on the night Jesus was betrayed, he told his disciples that whenever they reenacted that night of eating and drinking together, they were to eat the bread and drink the wine in remembrance of him. We gather tonight for that purpose. Memories, memories, memories — how important they are to our lives!

Authority And Freedom

On Using The Bible With Integrity

Philippians 3:12-16; 4:8-10

It happened in a large department store in Wilmington, Delaware. It was Christmas time. The store was filled with busy shoppers. At that moment I was standing around while members of my family made their purchases. I must have been dressed in my typical uniform of coat and tie because a teenage girl rushed up to me, papers in hand. She was obviously one of the temporary employees signed on for the holiday rush. She stood before me looking confused and hassled. "Are you authorized?" she asked, thrusting the papers toward me. Seeing my puzzlement, she repeated the question: "Are you authorized?" I hastily explained that I was not an employee but just a customer waiting around for my family. She quickly disappeared into the crowd, but her question remained with me. "Are you authorized?"

This is a question faced by everyone who stands up to preach. When churches ordain ministers, they authorize them to proclaim the gospel. Preaching consists of reading some words from the Bible and then adding some words of our own. We base what we say on the Bible. I have a question addressed to all of us who do that audacious thing we call preaching. While the question is especially relevant for preachers who have been authorized by some church to preach the gospel, it is not for preachers only. All Christians quote the Bible, at least now and then, in support of what they believe. We, in effect, say that the Bible authorizes us to believe and speak as we do. The question, then, is this: Is it possible to use the Bible with consistency and integrity as our authority? My half-serious answer is that it is possible but seldom achieved. When it happens, it is a cause for celebration.

Some time ago I participated in the questioning of a young candidate for ordination. He informed us that he believed in the inerrancy of Scripture. I remarked that he must surely believe that women should keep silent in the churches, 1 Corinthians 14:34. "Oh, no," he replied, "not at all." He then proceeded for several minutes to compare texts, to give contextual interpretations, and otherwise to show that this passage did not mean what it says. I exaggerate only a bit when I say that when he had finished, one would almost think that the Apostle Paul was urging women to speak up in church anytime they wanted to!

Let me say at once that my purpose here is not to engage in fundamentalist bashing. Liberals are also gifted in performing miracles of interpretation. A favorite sermon among us is based on Matthew 25:31-46. Here Jesus speaks of the Last Judgment when all will be judged by whether they have visited prisoners, fed the hungry, and clothed the naked. We are then exhorted to meet human need as an expression of our religious commitment. In the midst of all this, verses 41 and 46 are sometimes totally ignored or passed over so lightly as to be effectively dismissed. These verses have Jesus teaching the everlasting punishment of those who do not visit the sick or prisoners or feed the hungry. My point here has to do with consistency. In the story that Jesus told, the ethical teachings are inseparable from the notion that those who do not live by them will be punished forever. If it is true that those indifferent to human misery are to be sent to a never-ending hell, shouldn't that point be emphasized? Now liberals generally do not believe in eternal retribution for the unrighteous. It would not be nice for God to toss sinners into the everlasting flames, and for liberals above all else, God must be nice. They do believe that Jesus is the supreme religious and moral authority. Jesus is frequently quoted as if his word on the matter is final. If Jesus says it, it is true. If he is not to be believed when he teaches the everlasting torment of the wicked, why is he to be believed when he teaches us about other things? Why should we regard him as authoritative when he urges us to help those in trouble? What does make a teaching worthy of belief? Confusion frequently reigns. Liberals often preach as if the words and deeds of Jesus are authoritative above all else. They also find ways to ignore, avoid, or otherwise explain away what is not acceptable.

Some time ago I heard a minister preach a stewardship sermon. He used the story of the householder and the unjust tenants who not only refused to pay their rent but killed the servants who were sent to collect (Matthew 21:33-46). Finally, the householder sent his own son, who was likewise killed. Jesus asked what the householder would do when he returned. The answer was that he would put the tenants to a miserable death and let out the vineyard to other tenants who would produce fruit and pay their rent. Jesus does not take issue with the private exercise of capital punishment by the householder. Instead he suggests that God might act in a similar fashion and give the kingdom to a people who would be more faithful. What struck me is that when the minister came to the verse about putting the wicked tenants to a miserable death, he skipped over it completely without a comment. It was as if it were not there at all.

Or consider the matter of divorce. Here I find religious people of all persuasions doing a song and dance around the plain words of Jesus. In Matthew (5:32; 19:9) Jesus is reported to allow divorce only on grounds of adultery. In Mark (10:11-12) and Luke (16:18) Jesus does not allow any grounds for divorce. Moreover, anyone who remarries after divorce commits adultery. And is divorce permitted only for men? Matthew and Luke seem to say so. Mark apparently speaks of women and men alike. All three Gospels agree that marriage to or by a divorced person involves adultery.

What are we to do with these words? Well, we can call in the scholars who may tell us that it is Matthew, not Jesus, speaking when divorce is allowed on grounds of adultery. Whoever said it, are we to understand that adultery is a basis for divorce but that cruelty and abandonment are not? Mark and Luke may represent Jesus himself, who did not allow divorce for any reason. Ah, but, say the exegetes, we are not to take that ideal as a law to be obeyed in every case. It has to be adapted to circumstances. If that is the case, maybe the ideal of loving our neighbor as ourselves ought not to be taken as a principle to be lived by in every case either. Maybe that too is an impossible ideal. Maybe feeding the hungry and visiting the sick is too much to ask too. Where do we draw the line with respect to what is required, expected, and possible? What is mere strenuous idealism, an impossibly high guide to life that must be adapted to circumstances? And what about this business of remarriage by the divorced always involving adultery? All three Gospels agree that Jesus said that. That surely implies ideas about the importance of sexual union that is foreign to modern ears. Is there any way to interpret these texts as a final authority about marriage and divorce that is consistent with all the texts and with an enlightened responsible moral conscience today?

Now if we look at Matthew 10:8, we find Jesus sending out the apostles with the instruction that they are to raise the dead and cast out demons. I like to confound students by asking them how these programs are going in their churches. All churches claim to continue the ministry of the apostles. Why, then, do we not have ministries of casting out demons and raising the dead? Jesus said plainly we should.

My experience is that conservatives and liberals alike find themselves muddling through in order to come out with some kind of wisdom about life that will work. Nevertheless, nearly all Christian interpretations, though they contradict each other right and left, end up by claiming that they have discovered what Jesus really meant. Don't we all claim to have both Jesus and the Bible, when rightly interpreted, on our side?

Is it possible to use the Bible as an authority with consistency and integrity? Or do we end up with some sleight of hand by which we fool ourselves into believing that we do, while denying with the right hand what we have said on the left? It is a complex, subtle, slippery, and difficult matter, as I have discovered when trying to be consistent and to maintain integrity myself.

At this point I should let you in on a discovery I have made about the way the Bible is interpreted. In a fit of ambitious overstatement, I am prepared to say that in the last analysis only two rules of interpretation apply in actual use.

1. *Nobody allows the Bible to teach as authoritative truth for today what is believed to be either untrue or immoral.*
2. *Every Christian finds what the Bible teaches as authoritative truth for today to be identical with what he or she believes to be true and right.*

You will understand that I deliberately engage here in a bit of wild exaggeration with tongue in cheek to make a serious point. The first principle says that when we come across something in the Bible that we confidently believe to be wrong, we find ways to take the authority out of it. Fundamentalists do it as well as liberals. A century and a half ago many preachers in the North and South taught that slavery was an acceptable institution because the Bible approves it. No one that I know of does so today, not even biblical inerrantists. Likewise, the Bible was used a century ago to oppose granting women the right to vote. No one does so now. How do we explain this? Has the Bible changed? No, of course not. Our views of right and wrong have changed. As a result, not even those who believe the Bible is verbally inspired quote it to justify slavery or to deny the right of women to vote.

The second principle says that when we have completed our interpretation of Scripture, lo and behold, it agrees with us. The Bible has the same views of God, morality, and the meaning of life as we do. Take the issue of homosexuality — a hot issue in the church today. Conservatives believe that the practice of homosexuality is just plain wrong. They find that the Bible teaches that clearly. Of course, I do not hear them saying that homosexuals should be put to death, but Leviticus does (20:13). Neither do I hear fundamentalists urging that stubbornly disobedient sons should be stoned to death, but Deuteronomy teaches that (21:18-21).

A good many liberals these days have rethought the matter. They now think that a loving, faithful relationship between two men or two women is permissible. They look again at the Bible. Guess what? They conclude that those texts in Leviticus and Romans do not condemn loving, monogamous gay sex after all. They mean something else. Interestingly enough, both groups end up saying that they are only reporting what the Bible teaches, when rightly interpreted. Observing this, I can only wonder what is going on here. I think my two principles hold.

We could go on to give other examples. Let me pause and ask my initial question again: Is it possible to use the Bible consistently and with integrity? The answer, I think, is yes. I want to show how that is possible. I propose two principles.

1. We must take responsibility for what we believe. It is we who decide what in the Bible is right, true, good, and beautiful. By our choice and commitment we determine what is worthy of acceptance and practice in our day. Let us be honest about what we do. I put this in a little summary statement: *The text of the Bible may have the first word and the next to last word, but the interpreter has the last word, and it is the last word that finally counts.* So let us acknowledge that as interpreters **we** decide what is true, honorable, just, pure, lovely, gracious, excellent, and worthy of praise (Philippians 4:8). We should think on these things and devote ourselves to them.

2. We should honestly say that we accept as authoritative in Scripture only what we judge to be the highest and best that it teaches. And we take the highest and best in the Bible as authoritative only because it is supremely good. It appears to be unsurpassably excellent. We follow the highest and best in Scripture because we have not been able to find anywhere else in this world anything better. The highest and best in the Bible is worthy of our deepest devotion. At its center the Bible witnesses to a Creative and Gracious Love that brought the world into being. It calls upon us to respond by loving each other and by cooperating with God to increase justice and joy in the world. That vision of life is excellent indeed.

As Christians we believe that the truth most conducive to the quest for human fulfillment is identical with what we take to be most excellent in the biblical witness. That truth is unsurpassed by anything else we know from any source. So we continue to look to the traditions of ancient Israel and the early Church for the message most urgently needed today. We continue to look there because looking elsewhere has not yielded so rich a harvest of wisdom about life. We confess Jesus as the Christ because he is and has disclosed the Word that is nothing other than saving truth for us. We are Christians because it is to that tradition we turn, are compelled to turn, have no choice but to turn and return to, to argue with, to revise, to doubt and to reject, to transform and reinterpret, to be judged and transformed by. We read the Bible as Holy Scripture because of its unexcelled power to provide wisdom and a way of living that promises to actualize the finest that life — the gift of that Ultimate Mystery — offers.

In the text of the day, Saint Paul acknowledges that he has not yet attained perfection. He commits himself to pressing on toward the goal in response to the upward call of God in Jesus Christ. He urges us to do the same. He further exhorts us to cling to whatever is true, honorable, pure, lovely, gracious, excellent, and worthy of praise in pursuit of that calling. It is from the Bible that we have learned these very things. Let us hold on to that and only that.

A church can authorize us preachers and stamp our credentials. We determine whether we will use that authorization with competence and integrity. It is no trouble for any Christian to quote chapter and verse of the Bible as an authority. It is not so easy to do so with consistency. If you do not approve of my method of interpreting Scripture, I urge you to find your own way of integrity as you seek authorization for what is true, excellent, and deserving of praise.

Holding On And Pressing On

Philippians 3:8-16; 4:8

Sometimes we Baptists make jokes about ourselves. We say that wherever two Baptists gather, they will have three opinions. This diversity springs from some things we cherish. We emphasize the freedom of individuals to interpret Scripture for themselves under the guidance of the Spirit. If you turn individuals loose to think for themselves, different conclusions will follow. Back in the 1920s when the dispute between the fundamentalists and the modernists was at its height, Baptists were prominent in both camps, and many took extreme positions. Baptists were found all over the map then. They still are on a lot of theological and ethical issues.

E. Y. Mullins once wrote that Baptist distinctiveness could be summed up in the idea of the competence of the individual soul in matters of religion. This may not be a complete definition. It leaves out the community dimension. It omits the importance of the local congregation in which believers seek together to be the people of God. Nevertheless, if we combine the freedom and equality of individuals with an emphasis on the present activity of the Holy Spirit, we can go a long way toward understanding what Baptists have stood for over the centuries.

Of course, we share a great many beliefs in common with all Christians. In particular, we agree with other Protestants in giving special importance to the priority of Scripture over tradition. Likewise, we are Protestant in stressing salvation by grace through faith and not by works. Finally, with other Protestants we hold to the priesthood of all believers. We reject a special priesthood with powers that other believers don't have. Beyond that we have our distinctive way of being Protestant Christians. *And much that sets us apart follows from emphasis on the individual person and the local congregation living in the freedom of the Spirit.*

Look at some of our distinctive beliefs: the autonomy of the local congregation, believer's baptism, separation of church and state, and a strong doctrine of the priesthood of all believers. At the heart of all this is the conviction that all you need to have a full and complete church is a group of people with faith in the God of Jesus present to us through the Holy Spirit here and now. Nothing beyond the local congregation is necessary to constitute a valid church. The present activity of the Holy Spirit connects us to Christ and makes us an authentic part of the universal community of believers. Each congregation can do anything and everything that is necessary to its functioning. It governs itself. It calls and can ordain its own ministers. Gathered congregations must be free to determine for themselves what is true and right in matters of religion. The state must not interfere with the free exercise of personal liberty in matters of faith. To join this fellowship through the rite of baptism, you must make a personal confession of faith. All congregations are in principle equal to all others and free to be and to do what the Spirit dictates. All believers in a congregation are in principle equal to all other members and are free to follow the leading of the Spirit as they all together in that gathered community seek to know and to do the will of God. Individuals and congregations living in the freedom of the Spirit here and now — that is the heart of it.

Allowing for some oversimplification, it was something like this that came to define the Baptist way of being a Protestant Christian in the sixteenth and seventeenth centuries. But here we are now at the beginning of the twenty-first century. We sing a hymn containing a line that reads, "New occasions teach new duties; time makes ancient good uncouth" (James Russell Lowell). What does our past have to do with our present and our future? Any time we celebrate a milestone in our community life, this question becomes especially important. We treasure our past accomplishments, but is the past enough to guide us today and tomorrow? Does the future require of us new duties for new occasions? Has ancient good been made uncouth by the passage of time?

I believe the Apostle Paul gives us the clue we need. In his letter to the Philippians, he came to grips with the call of the future in the light of his present state as it had been shaped by his past. We can sum up his advice in the idea of "holding on" and of "pressing on." The past has given us something precious. So let us "hold true to what we have attained." But we are not yet perfect. We have not arrived finally. The future calls us to new achievement. So we need to forget what lies behind in order to strain forward to the goal that lies ahead. Let us, then, press on for the prize of the upward call of God in Christ Jesus. Paul suggests that maturity in living as a Christian involves "holding on" and "pressing on."

Yes, that gives us a clue. It also defines a difficulty. Much of the tension and conflict we feel in our churches can be located right here. When is it important to hold on to what we have attained already? When is it necessary to forget what lies behind in order to press on toward the goal we have not yet reached? What I want to do now is to lay out more specifically some problems we face in finding our way between "holding on" and "pressing on." In particular, I want to illustrate two forms this difficulty takes in our local church and in our life together as Baptists. What is true of Baptists, however, is also true in the life of all other churches and denominations.

The first is the challenge of embracing novelty without losing identity. "New occasions teach new duties; time makes ancient good uncouth." But if so, what happens to old truths and old duties? If we embrace too much novelty, will we not lose our identity? How much of the new can we add without ceasing to be what we have been? Let me illustrate this by reference to the authority of the Bible. Baptists look to the Scriptures as an indispensable source of truth. No problem has been more acute in the last two centuries than trying to remain loyal to the Scriptures when ancient truth begins to sound uncouth. Examples are easy to find.

A century and a half ago Baptists split over the question of slavery. The problem was that the slaveholders had all the good passages. The Old Testament authorizes slavery (Leviticus 25:44-46), and the New Testament assumes it without rejecting it. Abolitionists could not find a single verse condemning slavery. They had to resort to the larger principles of justice, freedom, and equality. Yet nobody today defends slavery, regardless of their view of biblical authority. We have in this case successfully pressed on.

Science has posed serious questions about the truth of Genesis. Is the biblical account of creation compatible with the theory of evolution? A prominent fundamentalist wrote some years ago that he had often seen a circus performer ride two horses at one time. But he remarked that he had never observed this being done when the horses were going in opposite directions. His point was that the Bible and evolution are not compatible. Christians still debate the issue. Many of us have found it possible to hold on to the old truth that God created all life and at the same time accept Darwin's theory about how it might have happened.

Christians are deeply divided today over homosexuality. Many conservatives quote Leviticus and Romans in support of the view that sexual love between persons of the same sex is forbidden. Some liberals contend that we have misunderstood those passages. Properly understood, they say, Scripture does not forbid faithful, monogamous unions between two men or two women. What is important, say these liberals, is the meaning a relationship has for the two people involved and their fidelity to each other. Conservatives point out that Leviticus 20:13 is pretty plain. But liberals note that Leviticus 20:13 not only condemns the practice but says the two men should be put to death. If we follow that verse in making homosexuality wrong, then should we not follow it in defining the punishment? But is any conservative urging that we kill gay men? And if we follow Leviticus 20:13 on homosexuality, shall we also follow Deuteronomy 21:18-21 regarding the treatment of disobedient sons? The prescription is that obstinate male children are to be stoned to death. How shall we interpret the Bible in these matters?

The issue of sexism and the role of women divides the church today. Many passages in the New Testament make women subordinate to men. They are told to keep silent in church (1 Corinthians 14:34); they are forbidden to exercise authority over men because Eve not Adam was deceived in the Garden of Eden (1 Timothy 2:11-14). On and on we could go. For many women and for many men, these verses have to be seen as reflecting the culture of that period and are without authority today. The larger truths of Scripture require full equality of the sexes in the churches and in society.

A few years ago a seminary student was teaching an adult class on the Lord's Prayer in a Baptist church. He suggested that we might better refer to God as our Parent rather than as our Father. Or at least we might speak of God as Mother as well as Father. He was jumped on immediately by some women in the class. They said we need to hold on to the old ways. Now I am sure that some of the men were taking great satisfaction in all this. They were glad the women were saying what they themselves felt. How is the proper way to speak of God? I have learned to speak of God without using any pronouns at all. But is that the right way to go about it? What do we do with all those old hymns we love that are full of sexist language? How can we embrace novelty without losing our identity and becoming something we have never been before? When do we need to press on toward the new instead of holding on to the old? It is not an easy question to answer.

The second problem has to do with the tension between seeking inclusiveness and maintaining intensity. The more you are willing to consider the beliefs of others as valid as yours, the less fervor you are likely to have for either set. The people most fanatically devoted to ideas and ideals are those who consider themselves to be in possession of absolute truth. How can a community be inclusive of people of contrary beliefs without losing intensity of devotion to a single truth about things? Let me illustrate.

Baptists in the past have insisted on believer's baptism. It is the right way to do it. It embodies the proper understanding of New Testament teachings on the subject. Yet most Christian churches baptize infants. They do so for good theological reasons. Think about it this way. Is entering the church more like being born into a family or more like getting married? If you think it is like being born into a family, you can support infant baptism. At birth you already belong to the family, and you are given the family name. If you think entering the church is more like getting married, you will support believer's baptism. Like marriage, becoming a Christian involves a personal commitment that only you can make. You can make a good theological case for both of these interpretations. So what are we Baptists to do? Should we admit people into our churches who were baptized as infants without requiring them to be baptized again? Should we hold on to the old exclusive truth or press on to a more inclusive outlook? But if both practices are equally valid, can we be as intensely devoted to its value as we could if we held that only believer's baptism is right? Do we dilute our faith by trying to become inclusive?

The very day I was writing this I got a letter from a good friend who was the pastor of a very liberal Baptist church in a nearby state. The church has an identity problem. Who are they? They are Baptists but quite unlike any other Baptists in the vicinity. Baptists who move there from other places attend once and are shocked by the theology they hear. Sometimes this church is suspected of being more like Unitarians. They want to be modern, ecumenical, inclusive, and liberal in outlook. How can they be true to their heritage and yet be open to the future? What does "holding on" and "pressing on" mean for them? My friend included a proposal soon to be voted on that includes two parts. First is the recommendation that they maintain their American Baptist affiliation but also join with the United Church of Christ. They would practice both infant baptism and believer's baptism depending on the preference of those involved. The second proposal is to change their name from "Second Baptist Church" to "Christ Ecumenical Church." That may be a wise move for them. But as they become more "ecumenical," will they not necessarily be less "Baptist"? In order to be more inclusive, do you lose intensity of devotion to some single ideal way of existing? What are the trade-offs to be measured?

What is the conclusion of the matter? In the church, we live between the past and the future. As Paul says, we are not perfect, but forgetting what lies behind, we strive forward toward the goal of the high calling of Christ. Yet in moving toward the new and the better, we must not turn loose of what is still good. So we live in tension between "holding on" and "pressing on." But how do we decide when to forget the past and embrace the new future that beckons? Paul also gives us a clue here. His last word is this: "Finally ... whatever is true, whatever is honorable, whatever is just, whatever is pure, whatever is lovely, whatever is gracious, if there is any excellence, if there is anything worthy of praise, think about these things." He does not give us any answers about what is true, good, and beautiful. He does give us some standards of measurement. As we employ them we must remember that what once was best may not be most excellent in the circumstances we face today. We have to decide afresh in every new generation. Nothing is necessarily good just because it is old. Nothing is necessarily better because it is new. We have to decide today in our own particular situation what is best for us here and now. What is superior for one congregation may not be preferable for another in different circumstances. And be assured that we will not always agree.

In seeking to be mature, we need to embrace novelty that is helpful without losing our identity. We need to become a more inclusive community without losing intensity of devotion to the truth as we see it. Each congregation must make those choices for itself. Each person must make those choices for himself or herself. As we do so, we will be living out something that is basic to our Baptist heritage — belief in the competence of congregations and of individuals living in the freedom of the Spirit in quest of the pure and the lovely. In that pursuit of maturity and excellence, we will live in the tension between forgetting the past and remembering what is good in it. In the freedom of the Spirit we hold on, and we press on. That surely is one conviction that any two Baptists with three opinions on most topics can always agree on.

www.ingramcontent.com/pod-product-compliance
Lightning Source LLC
Chambersburg PA
CBHW061306110426
42742CB00012BA/2072